Fashion Your Ow

THE SIMPLE WAY

Fourth Edition

CONNIE AMADEN-CRAWFORD

Published by Amaden-Crawford Inc.
P.O. Box 370
Hansville, Washington 98340
Phone: 360-638-2629
Fax: 360-638-0296
Email: fashionpatterns@centurytel.net
Web: www.fashionpatterns.com

PREFACE

Pants are a style of clothing that covers the lower torso and encircles each leg. Pants are styled in any length and width, and ususally include details such as a waistband, zipper opening, pockets, and cuffs.

In the late 19th century, the word "pants" was first used as a colloquial term for items worn by men and boys. Today, it is and all-inclusive term for any type of trouser, breeches, slacks, or jeans for both children and adults.

During the 1930's, well-known actresses, such as Katherine Hepburn and Marlene Deitrich, wore slacks and helped popularize this style of clothing for women. At that time women wore pants for sport activities such as horseback riding and bicycling. History continued to influence women's fashion when the women working in factories in World War II wore pants regularly. From the 1950's and 1960's women's pants continued to grow in popularity and became common items in wardrobes. Today, women's pants are more popular than ever and are worn for sportswear, casual wear, business wear, and evening wear.

I am pleased to write a book that simplifies how to draft and design your own pants. After many years of working in the garment industry and teaching fashion design at the college level, I saw a need for a book that contained simple steps and clear illustrations.

This book promises to guide a beginner or experienced clothier in:
- creating a basic pants pattern for average and mature figures
- creating various pant styles, simple to complicated
- designing various pant details such as pockets and waistbands
- simplifying pant sewing and construction

This book should enable anyone to draft and design their own pants or a friend's... "the simple way."

Connie Amaden-Crawford

DEBORAH MEYER, FASHION ILLUSTRATOR

Fourth Edition, Copyright © 2006 by Amaden-Crawford Inc.
Third Edition, Copyright © 2004 by Amaden-Crawford Inc.
Second Edition, Copyright © 2001 by Amaden-Crawford Inc.
Second Printing, June, 2002 by Amaden-Crawford Inc.
First Edition, Copyright © 1991 by Amaden-Crawford Inc.

LIBRARY OF CONGRESS CATALOG NUMBER TX 3-217-028

Published by Amaden-Crawford Inc.
Hansville, Washington - USA
www.fashionpatterns.com   360-638-2629
Printed in China

CONTENTS

PANT MEASUREMENT CHART

STANDARDIZED MEASUREMENT CHART

THIS CHART MAY BE USED WHEN NEEDING TO DRAFT PANTS
FOR MISSY AND PETITE STANDARD MEASUREMENTS

SIZE	C.F. WAIST TO ANKLE	S.S. WAIST TO ANKLE	C.B. WAIST TO ANKLE	FRONT HIP	BACK HIP	FRONT WAIST	BACK WAIST	CROTCH DEPTH
6 MISSY	37"	37-1/2"	36-3/4"	9-1/2"	9"	6-1/2"	6"	11"
8 MISSY	37-1/2'	38"	37-1/4"	9-3/4"	9-1/4"	6-3/4"	6-1/4"	11-1/4"
10 MISSY	38"	38-1/2"	37-3/4"	10"	9-1/2"	7"	6-1/2"	11-1/2"
12 MISSY	38-1/2"	39"	38-1/4"	10-3/8"	9-7/8"	7-3/8"	6-7/8"	11-3/4"
14 MISSY	39"	39-1/2"	38-3/4"	10-3/4"	10-1/4"	7-3/4"	7-1/4"	12"
16 MISSY	39-1/2"	40"	39-1/4"	11-3/4"	11-1/4"	8-1/4"	7-3/4"	12-1/4"
18 MISSY	40"	40-1/2"	39-3/4"	12-1/4"	11-3/4"	8-3/4"	8-1/4"	12-1/2"
3 PETITE	35-1/2"	36"	35-1/4"	8-3/4"	8-1/4"	6-1/4"	5-3/4"	10-1/2"
5 PETITE	35-3/4"	36-1/4"	35-1/2"	9"	8-1/2"	6-1/2"	6"	10-3/4"
7 PETITE	36"	36-1/2"	35-3/4"	9-1/4"	8-3/4"	6-3/4"	6-1/4"	11"
9 PETITE	36-1/4"	36-3/4'	36"	9-5/8"	9-1/8"	7"	6-1/2"	11-1/4"
11 PETITE	36-1/2"	37"	36-1/4"	10"	9-1/2"	7-3/8"	6-7/8"	11-1/2"
13 PETITE	36-3/4"	37-1/4"	36-1/2'	10-3/8"	9-7/8"	7-3/4"	7-1/4"	11-3/4"

PLEASE NOTE: ALL MEASUREMENTS INCLUDE EASE

PANT MEASUREMENT CHART

The following measurements are required for drafting a pant block

If using a live model, tie a string or twill tape around the model's waistline. Settle the tape where the model wants to wear the pants. Use the tape as a reference point for taking the following measurements. Make sure the model does not look down while taking the measurements. For best results, have the model remove shoes and wear only undergarments. Measurement accuracy aids a correct daft.

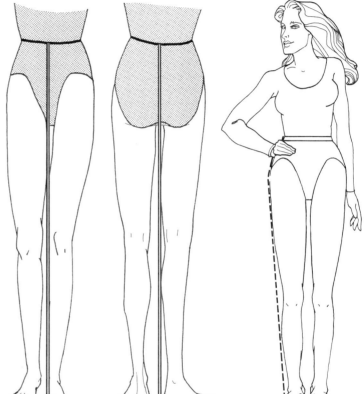

CENTER FRONT WAIST TO FLOOR _____

SIDE SEAM WAIST TO FLOOR _____

CENTER BACK WAIST TO FLOOR _____

HIGH HIP MEASUREMENT _____

LOW HIP MEASUREMENT _____

WAIST MEASUREMENT _____

CALF _____ **THIGH** _____

PANT INSEAM TO FLOOR _____
Use a tailors tape to teach between the legs and measure to the floor.

EASE AMOUNTS: The ease amount needed for the pants draft is figured and added within the text.

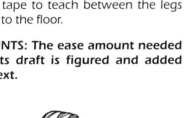

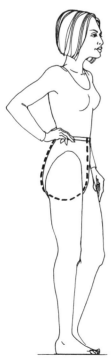

**TOTAL FRONT TO BACK
CROTCH SEAM LENGTH** _____
Hold the tape measure at center front waist, slip the tape between the legs and pull it fairly tight to center back. Read the measurement at the center back waist.

CROTCH SIDE SEAM DEPTH _____
While sitting, measure from the side seam waist, over the curve of the hip, and down to the chair.

NOTE: The **CHAIR DEPTH** and **INSEAM** measurement, ADDED TOGETHER, should be within ONE INCH of the SIDE SEAM MEASUREMENT.

WHY THE MEASUREMENTS MUST BE ACCURATE

This draft, literally, is controlled by the measurements you use. Using accurate measurements, and following the check points throughout the drafting process will aid the comfort and wearability of the finished pant. Incorrect measurements will result in an unbalanced pattern and a pant that twists and drapes incorrectly.

The following chart explains and illustrates the WAIST SLOPE, CHAIR DEPTH, AND OVERALL CROTCH. These measurements must be correct to ensure a properly fitting pants pattern.

1 **THE WAIST SLOPE (SHAPE):**
The distance from the floor to the waistline at CENTER FRONT, SIDE SEAM, AND CENTER BACK, controls the waist slope and length of the pants. (see the darkest lines on the illustration)

2 **THE CHAIR DEPTH:**
This measurement controls the amount of crotch depth that is drafted from the side seam/waist mark to your crotch level. Minimal ease will be added.

3 **THE OVERALL CROTCH:**
The overall crotch is determined by measuring the crotch from center front/waist through the legs to center back/waist. This measurement is necessary to have a check point for the front and back crotch draft.

4 **OTHER SHAPING CONSIDERATIONS:**
 ▪ **STOMACH FULLNESS** – This drafting method has been specially developed to allow for a fuller stomach.

 ▪ **FLAT TUSH** – The high hip and low hip measurement allow any "special shaping" needed for a flat tush. Also, a special back crotch shaping allows for the flat tush fit without creating back pant gapping.

 ▪ **LEGGING SHAPE** – Each customer has their own legging fullness preference. The hem circumference at the ankle controls this shape. We recommend between a 14" hem circumference (for less fullness) to a 20" hem circumference (for a good deal of fullness).

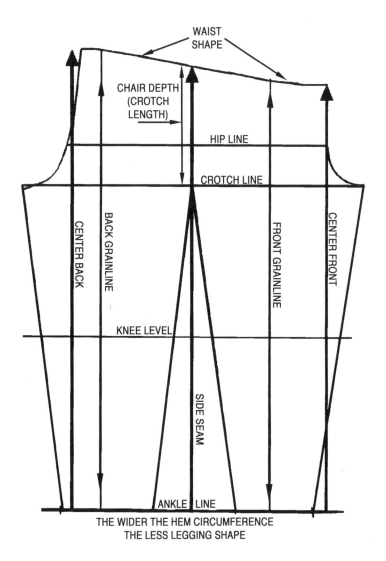

THE WIDER THE HEM CIRCUMFERENCE
THE LESS LEGGING SHAPE

DRAFTING THE BASIC FITTED PANT

This section contains the directions for creating a master pant pattern for petite and missy average sizes. The basic pant must be drafted and fitted before you can create other pant styles. In other words, this is the "key" to creating all other pant styles.

1   CUT A PIECE OF PATTERN
Cut a piece of pattern paper 50 inches long and 30 inches wide.

2   DRAW THE CENTER FRONT LINE
Draw a straight line 5 inches from the paper's right edge and the length of the center front waist to floor measurement, minus one inch. Crossmark the top (C.F. waist) and bottom (C.F. ankle) of this line.

3   DRAW THE ANKLE LINE
At the center front ankle crossmark (C.F. ankle), square and draw the ankle level.

4   DRAW THE HIPLINE
A From the center front line crossmark, measure down 7 inches and crossmark.

B At the 7-inch crossmark, square and draw the hipline.

5   FIGURE THE HIP MEASUREMENT
USING THE HIP MEASUREMENT, ADD THE EASE FOR THE PANT. **EASE: 1" for smaller figures, 1-1/2" for larger figures, and 2" for plus size figures.** Divide the hip measurement in half. Measuring from the center front hipline crossmark, mark one half of the total hip measurement, including the ease. Crossmark the end of this hipline measurement. (This is the center back position of the pant.)

6   DRAW THE CENTER BACK LINE
At the end of the hip distance crossmark, square and draw the center back line. Draw the line starting at the **ankle and measure UP to the waistline** using the center back to waist to floor measurement, minus 1".

7   DRAW THE SIDE SEAM LINE
A On the hipline, crossmark the side seam/hip position. Using the measurement from step 5, divide the hip measurement in half again. Place a crossmark **1/4 INCH TOWARD THE BACK.** (This makes the draft's front hip measurement 1/2 inch larger than the back hip measurement .)

FRONT HIP MEASUREMENT _____
BACK HIP MEASUREMENT _____

B At the side seam crossmark, **square and draw the side seam UP** from the ankle. Draw the line starting at the **ankle and measure UP to the waistline** using the side seam/waist to floor measurement, minus 1".

FIGURE HIP MEASUREMENT

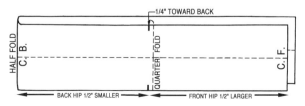

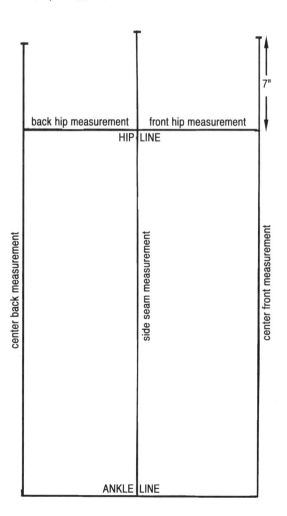

8 **DRAW THE WAISTLINE AND SHAPE THE UPPER SIDE SEAM**

A Draw a waistline by connecting the top of the center front line, the top of the side seam line, and the top of the center back line.

B Crossmark the waistline 3/4 inch IN on both sides of the side seam line. Draw a new side seam hip curve (using the hip curve ruler) from the 3/4 inch crossmark down to the original side seam about 2 inches above the hipline.

C On the waistline, crossmark UP 1/2 inch and IN 1/2 inch from the center back line

1. Draw a new center back line from the hipline up to the new center back corner.

2. Draw a new waistline from the new C.B. corner to the new side seam crossmark.

9 **FIGURE THE FRONT AND BACK WAIST MEASUREMENTS**

USING THE WAIST MEASUREMENT, ADD THE EASE FOR THE WAIST. **EASE: 1" for smaller figures, 1-1/2" for larger figures, and 2" for plus size figures.** Divide the waist measurement in half.

A On a scrap of paper mark 1/2 of the total waistline measurement, including the ease. Note the right crossmark as C.F. and the left crossmark as C.B.

B Fold the paper in half, matching the C.B. and C.F. crossmarks. Unfold the paper and crossmark the FOLD.

C Place a NEW CROSSMARK 1/4 INCH TOWARD THE BACK. (This makes the draft's front waist measurement 1/2 inch larger than the back waist measurement. See illustration).

FRONT WAIST 1/4 MEASUREMENT _____

BACK WAIST 1/4 MEASUREMENT _____

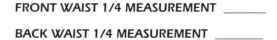

FIGURE WAIST MEASUREMENT

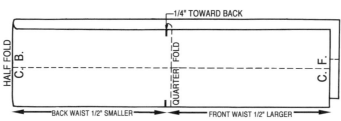

HALF FOLD · C.B. · BACK WAIST 1/2" SMALLER · QUARTER FOLD · 1/4" TOWARD BACK · FRONT WAIST 1/2" LARGER · C.F.

UP 1/2" · 3/4" · IN 1/2" · C.B. · C.F. · HIP LINE · Center Back · Side Seam · Center Front · ANKLE LINE

OPTIONAL: THE PLACING OF THE DARTS MAY BE COMPLETED AFTER STEP 20. THIS
WILL ALLOW ONE FRONT DART TO BE PLACED EXACTLY ON THE FRONT GRAINLINE.

10 FIGURE THE FRONT DART AMOUNTS

Measure from the center front waistline toward the side seam using the front waist quarter measurement. Lightly crossmark this position.

The distance between the new side seam and the quarter waist crossmark is the total front dart intake. For two darts, divide the amount in half.

FRONT DART(S) AMOUNT _____

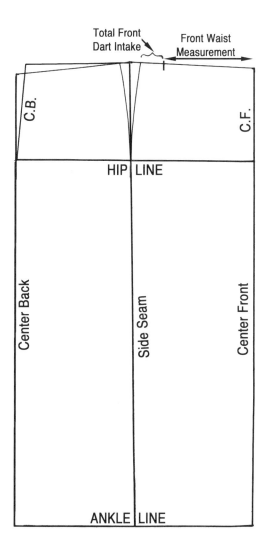

11 DRAW THE FRONT WAISTLINE DARTS.

A Place the first dart 3 inches IN from the center front line. Crossmark the width using the front dart amount

B Place the second dart 1-1/4 inches from the first dart and crossmark the front dart amount.

C Square and draw the center of each dart 3-1/2 inches long. Connect all points.
NOTE: Front dart lengths may vary, depending upon the design, but they should not be longer than 5 inches.

The placement of the front darts may be readjusted after Step 20 is completed. (SEE NOTE AT TOP OF PAGE.)

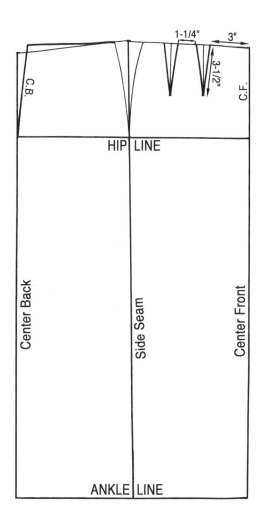

12 FIGURE THE BACK DART AMOUNTS.

Measure from the center back toward the side seam using the back waist quarter measurement. Crossmark this position.

The distance between the new side seam and the crossmark is the total back dart intake. For two darts, divide the amount in half. (Sometimes there may only be enough intake for one small dart.)

BACK DART(S) AMOUNT _____

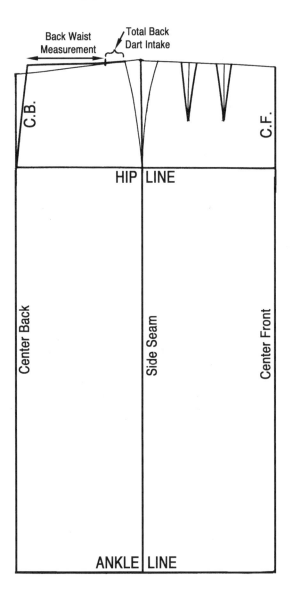

13 DRAW THE BACK WAISTLINE DARTS.

A Place the first dart 2-5/8 inches IN from the center back line. Crossmark the width using the back dart amount.

B Place the second dart 1-1/4 inches from the first dart and crossmark the back dart amount.

C Square and draw the center of each dart 5-1/2 inches long. Connect all points.

NOTE: Back dart lengths may vary, depending upon the design, but they should not be longer than 6 inches.

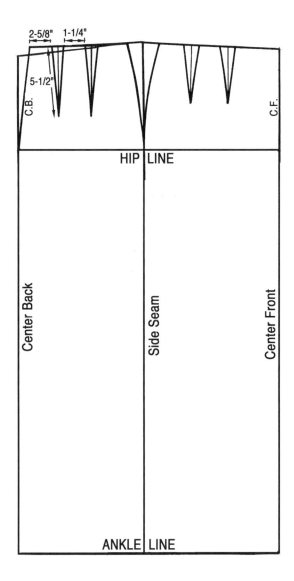

14 DRAW THE KNEE LINE

Measure from the ankle level to the hipline and divide this distance in half. At the halfway postition crossmark, square and draw in the knee line.

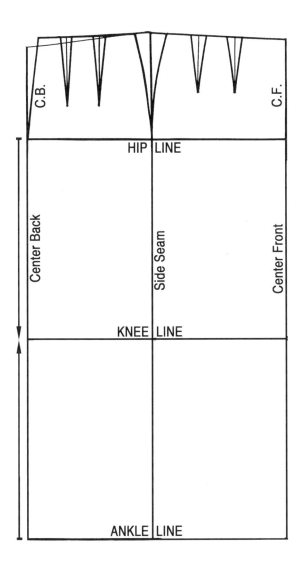

15 DRAW THE CROTCH LINE

From the top of the side seam line, measure down toward the knee level using the crotch depth measurement, plus ease.

EASE: 1/2" for smaller figures, 3/4" for larger figures, and 1" for plus size figures.

Crossmark this distance. Square and draw in the crotch line on this crossmark, extending the line several inches past the center front line and center back line.

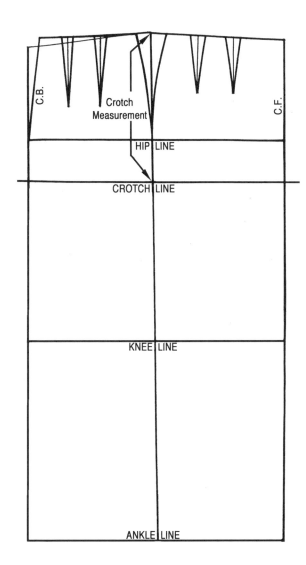

16 DEVELOP THE FRONT CROTCH CURVE

A Measure the distance from the side seam to the center front line. Divide this distance into FOUR EQUAL PARTS.

B Extend the crotch line out from the center front line using the quartered measurement. Crossmark.

C At the C.F./CROTCH intersection, draw an angled line 1-1/4 INCHES long. Crossmark the end of this line.

D Using a french curve ruler, draw a FRONT CROTCH CURVE that connects the CENTER FRONT LINE, touches the 1-1/4" CROSSMARK, and the CROTCH LINE (see illustration).

17 DEVELOP THE BACK CROTCH CURVE

A Measure the distance from the side seam to the center back line. Divide this distance into TWO EQUAL PARTS.

B Extend the crotch line out from the center back line using the divided back measurement. Crossmark.

C At the C.B./CROTCH intersection, draw an angled line 1-3/4 INCHES long (1-1/4 INCHES for FLAT TUSH). Crossmark the end of this line.

D Using a french curve ruler, draw a BACK CROTCH CURVE that connects the CENTER BACK LINE, touches the 1-3/4" CROSSMARK, and the CROTCH LINE (see illustration).

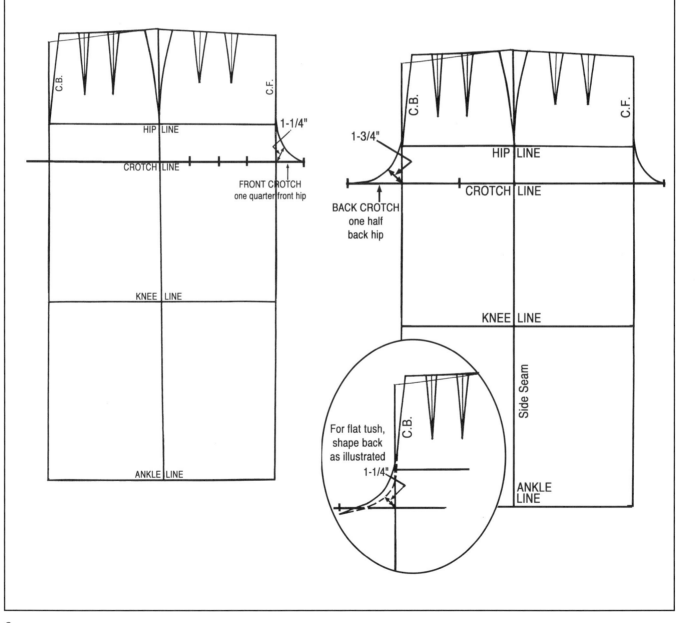

18 CHECK THE CROTCH SEAM LENGTH
On the pattern, measure the front and back crotch seam lengths. Add the two measurements together.

This measurement should equal the overall crotch length on the measurement chart. If these measurements do not match, add or subtract one fourth of the difference to the C.F. WAIST, the C.B. WAIST, the FRONT CROTCH INSEAM, and the BACK CROTCH INSEAM.

If the difference between the measurements is more than 1-1/2", an error was probably made in the original body measurement.

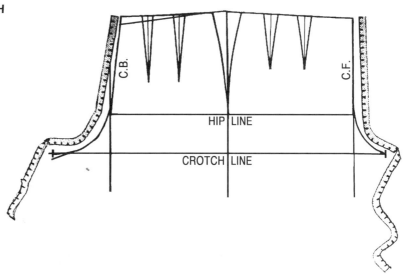

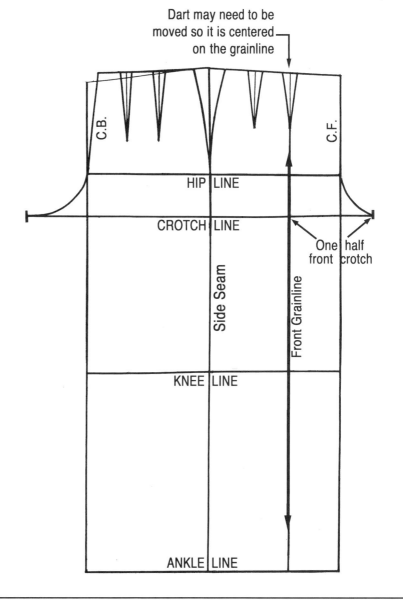

Dart may need to be moved so it is centered on the grainline

19 DRAW THE FRONT GRAINLINE
Divide in half the distance from the side seam to the end of the front crotch line. Square and draw a grainline at the halfway position, extending it from the waist to the ankle.

NOTE: The front darts may now be moved so that the dart closest to center front is centered on the front grainline. The second dart should be 1 1/4 inches from the first dart.

20 DRAW THE BACK GRAINLINE

Using the same measurement as the front, add 1/2 inch. Crossmark this new measurement from the side seam toward the back crotch. Square and draw the back grainline at this position, extending it from the waist to the ankle.

NOTE: The back darts are not readjusted with the grainline.

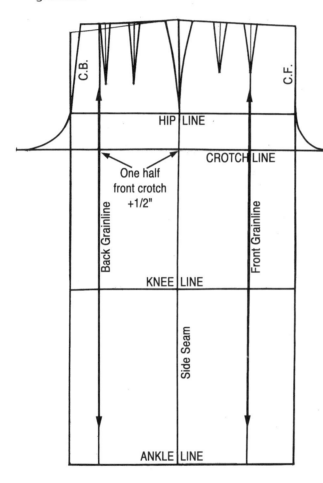

21 SELECT THE ANKLE WIDTH

A basic pant block uses an ankle width of 14 inches. (6-1/2 inches for the front and 7-1/2 inches for the back). Crossmark half of these measurements on each side of the grainline.

- 3-1/4 inches on both sides of the FRONT GRAIN-LINE.

- 3-3/4 inches on both sides of the BACK GRAIN-LINE.

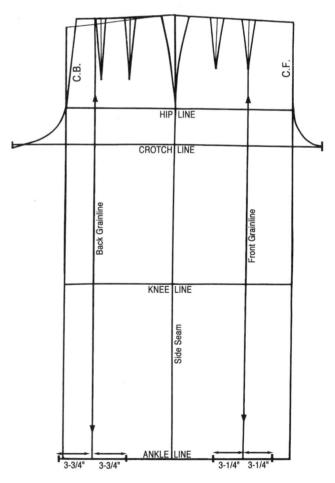

22 DRAW THE SIDE SEAM LEGGING

For both the front and the back: Draw a new line from the ankle crossmark to the side seam at the crotch level. (These lines are the new side seams.)

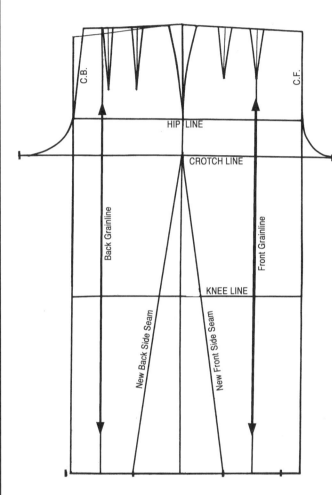

23 DRAW THE FRONT IN-SEAM LEGGING

A On the KNEE LEVEL, measure from the new front side seam to the front grainline. Extend this same measurement from the opposite side of the front grainline. Crossmark.

B Using a long ruler, connect the ankle crossmark to the knee level crossmark, and continue extending this line up to the crotch line.

C Using a hip curve ruler, blend the end of the front crotch line into the new in-seam as illustrated.

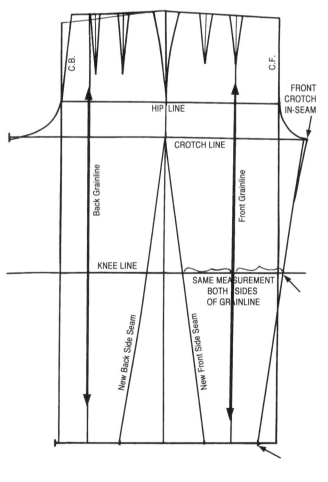

24 DRAW THE BACK IN-SEAM LEGGING

A On the KNEE LINE, measure from the new back side seam to the back grainline. Extend this same measurement from the opposite side of the back grainline. Crossmark.

B Using a long ruler, connect the back ankle crossmark to the knee lline crossmark and continue extending this line up to the crotch line.

C Using a hip curve ruler, blend the end of the back crotch line into the new inseam line as illustrated.

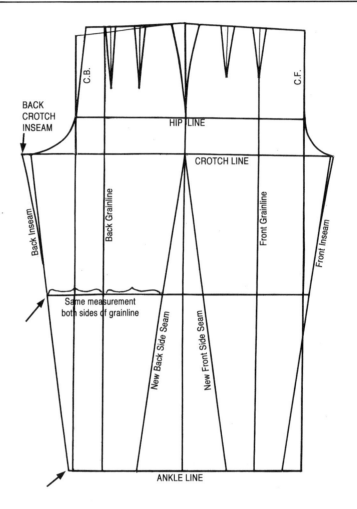

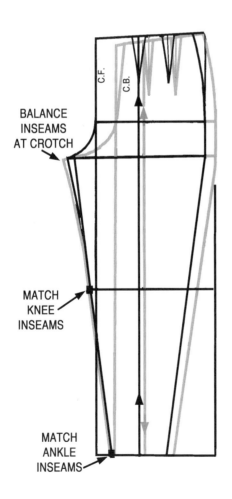

25 BALANCE THE FRONT AND BACK IN-SEAMS

A Pin the front and back to each other at the ankle in-seams and knee in-seams. (If the paper twists when these two positions are pinned to each other, an error was made during the drafting process or the pattern lines are not perfectly square.)

B When the in-seams are pinned in place, note the position of the back crotch in-seam and the front crotch in-seam. If these two positions do not match, divide the difference in half, mark.

C Using a hip curve ruler, reblend a new in-seam from the crotch to the knee level. This makes the front and back in-seams the same shape and length.

NOTE: If the divided distance is more than 3/8 inch, an error was made in the measurements and/or drafting process.

26 CUT THE PATTERN OUT

Add all appropriate seam allowances and cut the pattern out. Re-check the following areas:

- Inseam Balance – in-seams should be the SAME SHAPE AND LENGTH when the grainlines are parallel to each other.

- Side Seam Balance – side seams should be the SAME SHAPE AND LENGTH when the grainlines are parallel to each other.

- Mark all notches as illustrated.

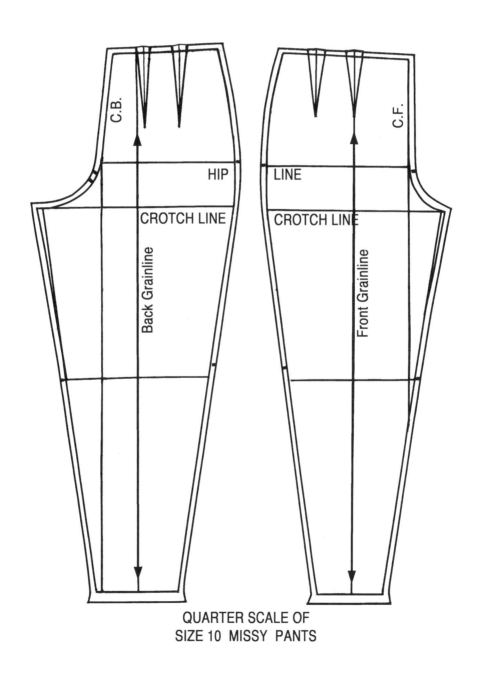

QUARTER SCALE OF
SIZE 10 MISSY PANTS

FINAL FITTING PROCEDURES

Complete the following steps of the sewing and fitting process. Mark any fitting changes on the pant muslin and transfer the changes onto your pattern. Please take special care when fitting the following areas:

LEGGING SHAPE: The pattern legging is shaped to give a better fit and decrease the "baggy" look. However, you may adjust it to your personal preference.

HIP SHAPE: The hip area may need extra fitting because of differences such as a high hip, flat buttocks, or low hip. If necessary, reshape the hip area to fit smoothly on your body. (see instructions below)

SEWING
1 Sew the pant out of muslin or an inexpensive fabric. Do not sew the pockets, do not sew any elastic casings.

CHECK FOR CORRECT FIT IN THE WAISTLINE AND CROTCH DEPTH
1 Put the pants on correct side out.

2 Tie a string or twill tape around the waistline where you want to wear the pants.

3 Evenly distribute the fullness around the waistline.

4 At the same time, adjust the pants crotch to a comfortable wearing position. Be sure to keep the pant "drape" straight up and down. Do not let the pants twist.

5 Mark the waistline with a pencil or felt tip pen. Transfer any changes to the pattern.

IF THE CROTCH DEPTH IS TOO LONG: Cut the pattern front and back on the HIP LINE. CLOSE the pattern evenly on this line in 1/2" increments.

IF THE CROTCH DEPTH IS TOO SHORT: Cut the pattern front and back on the HIP LINE. OPEN the pattern evenly on this line in 1/2" increments.

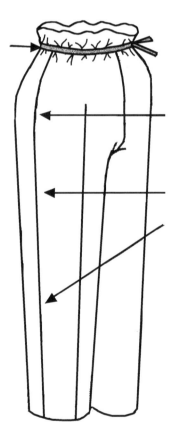

RESHAPE THE LEGGING AND HIP SIDE SEAM
Drape-fit the side seams to the shaping desired for each design.

IF THE HIP AREA IS PROTRUDING:
Pin the hip area to fit your body and desired shape.

IF THE LEGGING IS TOO LOOSE:
1 Pin and shape the side seam to your desired fit.
2 Then pin the inseam to your desired fit. (The inseam may not need any extra shaping.) Do not change the hem circumference. The pattern has the hem circumference you requested.

IF THE LEGGING IS TOO TIGHT:
1 Cut another muslin with a 1" seam allowance in the pant leg.
2 Pin and shape the side seam to your personal preference.
3 Pin and shape the in-seam to your personal preference.

PANT BLOCKS

When a manufacturer develops a new clothing line, one of the first demands is a set of foundation patterns (blocks). These foundation patterns should match the proportion, size, and fit of the target customers. This provides the designer and manufacturer with a consistant fit, silhouette, ease allowance, armhole size, waistline measurement, and desired length.

On the following pages are directions for drafting the most commonly used pant blocks needed for creating various designs.

FASHION JEANS BLOCK

The jeans block should be used to develop other styles that require a slimmer jeans fit.

1 Raise and crossmark the crotch line/inseam UP 1/2 inch and IN 1/2 INCH.

2 Crossmark center front and center back waists IN 1/2 inch.

3 Blend a new front and back crotch by connecting the new center front and center back waist crossmarks with the new crotch crossmarks.

4 At the ankle, crossmark the inseams and side seams IN 1 inch toward the grainlines.

5 Taper the legging from the new crotch crossmark to the new ankle crossmarks.

6 RE-FIGURE and DRAFT the waist darts into one dart for the front and one dart for the back.

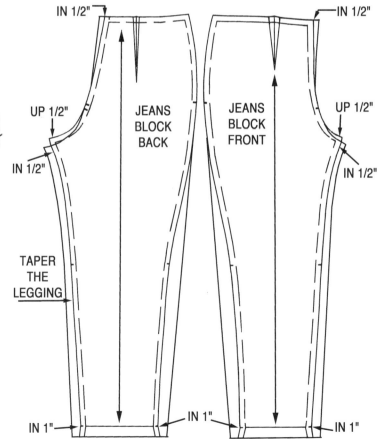

STIRRUP/STRETCH PANTS BLOCK

MEASUREMENT CHART
FOR STIRRUP STRETCH PANTS
These proportions have been based on 100% stretch
(see "Knit Fabric Characteristics" below)

C.F. to Floor (minus 6 inches) _____

S.S. to Floor (minus 6 inches) _____

C.B. to Floor (minus 6 inches) _____

Waist Measurement (no ease added) _____

Hip Measurement (minus 2 inches) _____

Crotch Depth (minus 1-1/2 inches) _____

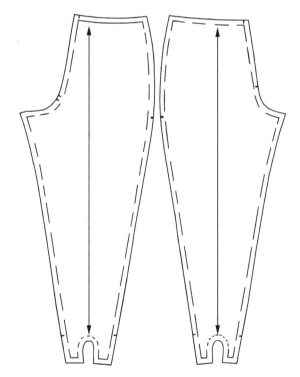

CHANGES IN DIRECTIONS FROM WOVEN
TO SIRRUP STRETCH PANTS

STEP #8-C
CHANGE TO: Crossmark UP 1 inch and IN 1 inch at center back waist and IN 1 inch at center front waist.

Step #10, 111, 12, and 13
No darts are developed. Skip these steps.

Step #26
Add stirrup design instead of a hem. (5" past ankle and shaped as illustrated)

KNIT FABRIC CHARACTERISTICS
A well constructed knit has stretch and recovery characteristics that provide "give" during the movement of the body. Stretch ratio is the amount of stretch (per inch) that occurs when a knit is stretched to its maximum width and/or length.

The measurements used for stirrup/stretch pants may vary, depending upon the stretch ratio of a fabric. Sometimes the measurements may only change in length and sometimes they may only change in width. Analyze each fabric on an individual basis.

KNIT FABRIC CLASSIFICATIONS
An important factor in working with knits is the direction of stretch – one way or two way. Most knits are either single or double knits. Knit fabrics stretch in varying amounts, but single knits usually stretch more than double knits, and are therefore less stable.

- **Stable/Firm Knits to Moderate Stretch Knits (18% to 25% stretch ratio on the crosswise grain)** These knits parallel the fit of woven fabrics and are NOT recommended for a strirrup stretch pant design. For example, double knits are usually limited in their amount of stretch and thus maintain their original shape too well.
- **Stretchy Knits to Super Stretch Knits (50% to 100% stretch ratio on the crosswise grain)** These knit fabrics are ACCEPTABLE and recommended for a strirrup/stretch pant design. Examples, such as a spandex or lycra, are lightweight, have power stretch properties, drape well, and are employed in body contouring designs.

BOYS AND GIRL'S PANT BLOCK

STYLING THE GIRL'S OR BOY'S PANT

Girls or boys pants are styled using the same methods as the women's patterns. Illustrated below are the pleated pant and the elastic waist pant for girls and boys. Other styles can be designed by following the women's pattern directions.

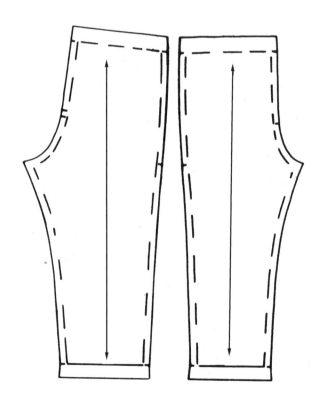

PATTERN DIFFERENCES FROM WOMEN'S TO GIRL'S/BOY'S PANTS

Measure and draft in the same manner as the average size missy/petite basic pant. However, because of a younger age, the measurements will vary greatly and the waistline slope will be similar to men's pants.

Step #4
CHANGE TO: Because all measurements are shorter in children's pants, the HIPLINE should be placed 4 inches down from the center front waist crossmark.

Step #8-B
CHANGE TO: Crossmark the waistline IN 3/8 inch on both sides of the side seam line.

Step #10, 11, 12, and 13
Typically, no darts are developed because elastic waistlines are almost always used. (Follow the directions for the GATHERED ELASTIC WAIST DESIGN to complete the girl's/boy's block.)

MEN AND OLDER PANT BLOCK

STYLING THE MAN'S OR OLDER BOY'S PANTS
Men's and Older Boys' pants are styled using the same methods as the women's patterns. Illustrated are the pleated pant and the elastic waist pant. Other styles can be designed by following the women's pattern directions.

PATTERN DIFFERENCES FROM WOMEN'S TO MAN's AND OLDER BOY'S PANTS
Measure and draft in the same manner as the average size missy/petite basic pant. However, because of men's stance, the measurements will be shorter at center front and longer at center back. Also, the crotch depth will be obviously shorter than women's.

Step #4
CHANGE TO: Due to a shorter crotch measurement, the HIPLINE will be placed 6 inches down from the center front waist crossmark.

Step #8-B
CHANGE TO: Crossmark the waistline IN 3/8 inch on both sides of the side seam line.

Step #8-C
CHANGE TO: Crossmark UP 3/4 inch and IN 3/4 inch from the center back line.

Step #15
Add 2 inches of ease to the crotch depth measurement.

Step #16-C
Draw an angle out 1-3/4 inch to blend the front crotch.
NOTE: This softer curve allows more room for the "jewels".

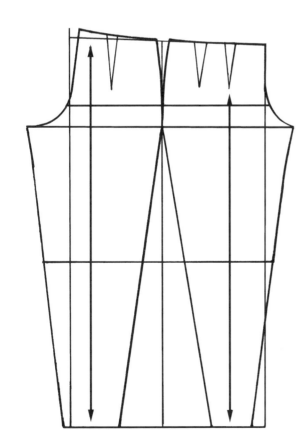

PANT DRAFT FOR THE MATURE FIGURE

MEASUREMENT CHART

For best results, wear undergarments and remove all shoes. Measure accurately, do not take your own measurements. Be careful not to move or look down while the measurements are taken. Tightly tie a wide string or twill tape around the waistline - where you want to wear your pant or skirt. Use the tape as a reference point for the following measurements. Double check these measurements.

DEFINITION OF WAISTLINE SLOPE: The distance from the hipline to the waistline at center front, side seam, and center back.

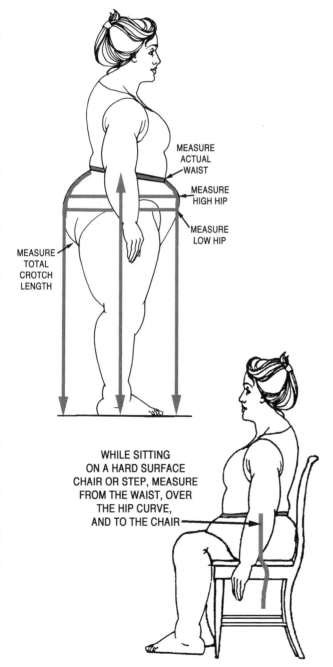

MEASURE ACTUAL WAIST

MEASURE HIGH HIP

MEASURE LOW HIP

MEASURE TOTAL CROTCH LENGTH

WHILE SITTING ON A HARD SURFACE CHAIR OR STEP, MEASURE FROM THE WAIST, OVER THE HIP CURVE, AND TO THE CHAIR

CENTER FRONT/WAIST TO FLOOR _____

SIDE SEAM/WAIST TO FLOOR _____

CENTER BACK/WAIST TO FLOOR _____

HIGH HIP MEASUREMENT _____
Measure about 3" below the front of the waistline tape (fullest part of the stomach).

LOW HIP MEASUREMENT _____
Measure the fullest part of the tush.

WAIST MEASUREMENT _____

CALF _____   **THIGH** _____

PANT INSEAM TO FLOOR _____
Use a tailors tape to teach between the legs and measure to the floor.

TOTAL FRONT TO BACK OVERALL CROTCH SEAM LENGTH _____
Hold the tape measure at center front waist, slip the tape between the legs and pull it fairly tight to center back. Read the measurement at the center back waist.

CROTCH/SIDE SEAM DEPTH _____
While sitting, measure from the side seam waist, over the curve of the hip, and down to the chair.

EASE AMOUNTS
The ease amount needed for the pants draft is figured and added within the text.

CHECKPOINT FOR MEASUREMENTS
The **CHAIR DEPTH** and **INSEAM** measurement, ADDED TOGETHER, should be within ONE INCH of the SIDE SEAM MEASUREMENT.

PANT DRAFT FOR THE MATURE FIGURE

As people age and/or add on body weight, their waistline slope may change and a full tush is usually replaced with a full stomach and high hip.

This draft creates a more accurate waistline slope and adjusts to the hip and stomach proportions of a fuller figure. The hip and crotch level are drafted parallel to the floor, creating a pant that drapes correctly without twisting.

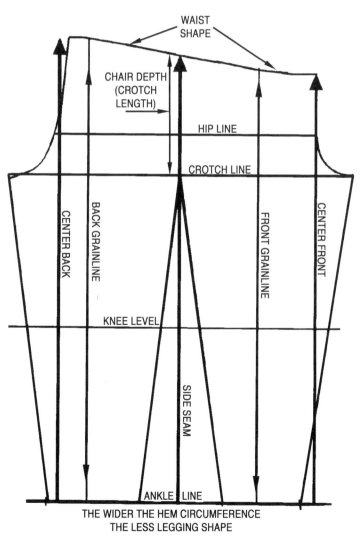

WAIST SHAPE

CHAIR DEPTH (CROTCH LENGTH)

HIP LINE

CROTCH LINE

CENTER BACK

BACK GRAINLINE

FRONT GRAINLINE

CENTER FRONT

KNEE LEVEL

SIDE SEAM

ANKLE LINE

THE WIDER THE HEM CIRCUMFERENCE
THE LESS LEGGING SHAPE

This section contains the directions for creating a master pattern for female mature figures. This basic pants block must be drafted and fitted before you can create other pant styles. Once completed, you can use the "Pant Styles" section to create other designs.

1 CUT A PIECE OF PATTERN
Cut a piece of pattern paper 50 inches long and 45 inches wide.

2 DRAW THE CENTER FRONT LINE
Draw a straight line 7 inches from the paper's right edge and the length of the center front waist to floor measurement, minus one inch. Crossmark the top **(C.F. waist)** and bottom **(C.F. ankle)** of this line.

3 DRAW THE ANKLE LINE
At the center front ankle crossmark (C.F. ankle), square and draw the ankle level.

4 DRAW THE HIPLINE
A From the center front line crossmark, measure down 7 inches and crossmark.

B At the 7-inch crossmark, square and draw the hipline.

5 FIGURE THE HIP MEASUREMENT
USING THE HIP MEASUREMENT, ADD THE EASE FOR THE PANT. **EASE: 1" for smaller figures, 1-1/2" for larger figures, and 2" for plus size figures**. Divide the hip measurement in half. Measuring from the center front hipline crossmark, mark one half of the total hip measurement, including the ease. Crossmark the end of this hipline measurement. (This is the center back position of the pant.)

6 DRAW THE CENTER BACK LINE
At the end of the hip distance crossmark, square and draw the center back line. Draw the line starting at the **ankle and measure UP to the waistline** using the center back to waist to floor measurement, minus 1".

7 DRAW THE SIDE SEAM LINE
A On the hipline, crossmark the side seam/hip position. Using the measurement from step 5, divide the hip measurement in half again. Place a crossmark **1/2 INCH TOWARD THE BACK**. (This makes the draft's front hip measurement 1 inch larger than the back hip measurement .)

FRONT HIP MEASUREMENT _____
BACK HIP MEASUREMENT _____

B At the side seam crossmark, **square and draw the side seam UP** from the ankle. Draw the line starting at the **ankle and measure UP to the waistline** using the side seam/waist to floor measurement, minus 1".

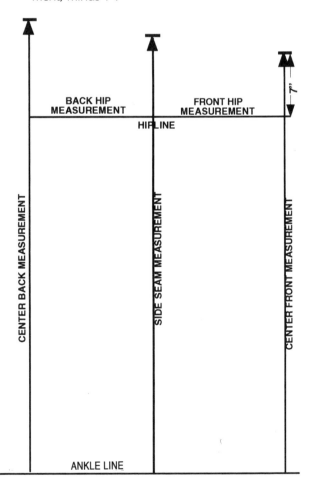

8 DRAW THE WAISTLINE AND SHAPE THE UPPER SIDE SEAM

A Draw a temporary waistline by connecting the top of the C.F. line, the top of the side seam line, and the top of the C.B. line.

B Crossmark the waistline **1/2 inch IN** on both sides of the side seam line. Draw a new side seam hip curve (using the hip curve ruler) from the 1/2 inch crossmark down to the original side seam about 2 inches above the hipline.

C On the waistline, crossmark **UP 1 inch** and **IN 3/4** inch from the C.B. line.
NOTE: Smaller figures will add only 1/2 inch. Figures with a "back porch" hip may need to add up to 2 inches. (See fitting instructions on page..... to accurately fit this waistline curve.)
  1 Draw a new C.B. line from the hipline up to the new C.B. corner.
  2 Draw a new waistline from the new C.B. corner to the new side seam.

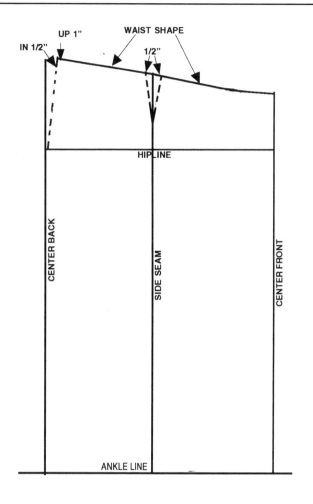

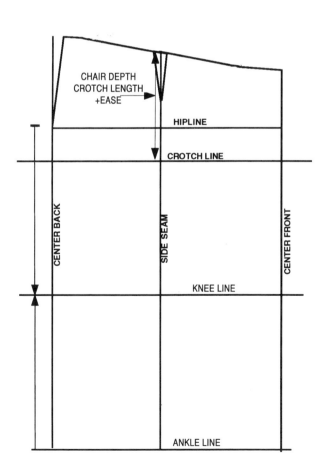

9 DRAW THE KNEE LINE
Measure from the ankle level to the hipline and divide this distance in half. At the halfway position, crossmark, square and draw in the knee level.

10 DRAW THE CROTCH LINE
From the top of the side seam line, measure down toward the knee level using the crotch depth measurement, plus ease.

EASE: 1/2" for smaller figures, 3/4" for larger figures, and 1" for plus size figures.

Crossmark this distance. Square and draw in the crotch line on this crossmark, extending the line several inches past the center front line and center back line.

11 DEVELOP THE FRONT CROTCH CURVE

A On the crotch line, measure the distance from the side seam to the center front line. Divide this distance into THREE EQUAL PARTS. NOTE: Divide this distance into quarters for smaller figures (48 inch hips and below.)

B Extend the crotch line out from the center front line using the 1/3 measurement. Crossmark.

C At the C.F./CROTCH intersection, draw an angled line 1-1/4 INCHES long. Crossmark the end of this line.

D Using a french curve ruler, draw a **FRONT CROTCH CURVE** that connects the CENTER FRONT LINE, TOUCHING THE 1-1/4" CROSSMARK, and the CROTCH LINE (see illustration).

12 DEVELOP THE BACK CROTCH CURVE

A Measure the distance from the side seam to the center back line. Divide this distance into TWO EQUAL PARTS.

B Extend the crotch line out from the center back line using the divided back measurement. Crossmark.

C At the C.B./CROTCH intersection, draw an angled line 1-3/4 INCHES long (1-1/4 INCHES for FLAT TUSH). Crossmark the end of this line.

D Using a french curve ruler, draw a **BACK CROTCH CURVE** that connects the CENTER BACK LINE, TOUCHING THE 1-3/4" CROSSMARK, and the CROTCH LINE (see illustration).

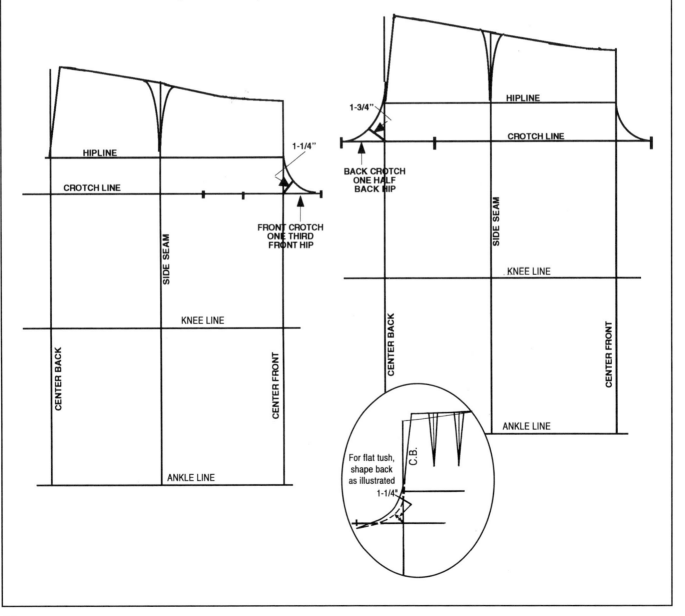

13 CHECK THE CROTCH SEAM LENGTH

On the pattern, measure the front and back crotch lengths. Add the two measurements together.

This measurement should equal the OVERALL CROTCH LENGTH on the measurement chart. If these measurements do not match, add or subtract one fourth of the difference to the C.F. WAIST, the C.B. WAIST, the FRONT CROTCH INSEAM, and the BACK CROTCH INSEAM.

If the difference between the measurements is more than 1-1/2", an error was probably made in the original body measurement.

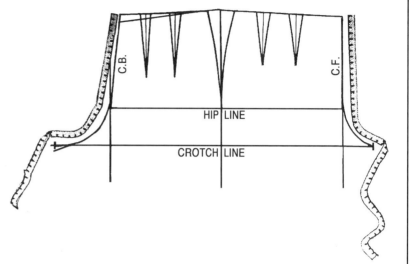

14 DRAW THE FRONT GRAINLINE

Divide in half the distance from the side seam to the end of the front crotch line. Square and draw a grainline at the halfway position. (Draw the grainline from the waist to the ankle.)

15 DRAW THE BACK GRAINLINE

Using the same measurement as the front, add 1/2 inch. Crossmark this new measurement from the side seam toward the back crotch. Square and draw the back grainline at the crossmark. (Draw the grainline from the waist to the ankle.

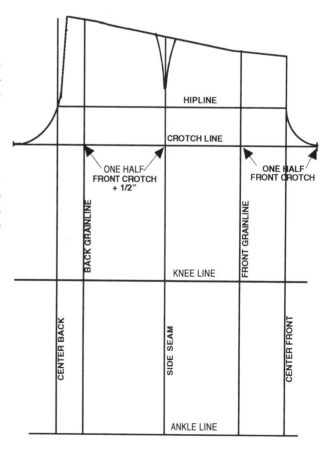

16 FIGURE THE FRONT AND BACK WAIST MEASUREMENTS

USING THE WAIST MEASUREMENT, ADD THE EASE FOR THE WAIST. **EASE: 1" for smaller figures, 1-1/2" for larger figures, and 2" for plus size figures.** Divide the waist measurement in half.

A On a scrap of paper mark 1/2 of the total waistline measurement, including the ease. Note the right crossmark as C.F. and the left crossmark as C.B.

B Fold the paper in half, matching the C.B. and C.F. crossmarks. Unfold the paper and crossmark the FOLD.

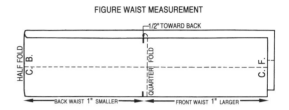

FIGURE WAIST MEASUREMENT

C Place a NEW CROSSMARK 1/2 INCH TOWARD THE BACK. (This makes the draft's front waist measurement 1 inch larger than the back waist measurement. See illustration).

FRONT WAIST 1/4 MEASUREMENT _____

BACK WAIST 1/4 MEASUREMENT _____

17 FIGURE THE FRONT DART AMOUNTS

Measure from the center front waistline toward the side seam using the front waist quarter measurement. Crossmark this position.

The distance between the new side seam and the quarter waist crossmark is the total front dart intake. (For two darts, divide the amount in half.)

FRONT DART(S) AMOUNT _____

18 DRAW THE FRONT WAISTLINE DARTS

A Place the first dart on the front grainline. Crossmark each side of the grainline half of the front dart amount.

B Place the second dart 1-1/2" (1-1/4" for smaller sizes) from the first dart and crossmark the front dart amount.

C Square and draw the center of each dart 4 inches long. Connect all points as illustrated.
NOTE: Front dart lengths may vary, depending upon the design, but they should not be longer than 5 inches.

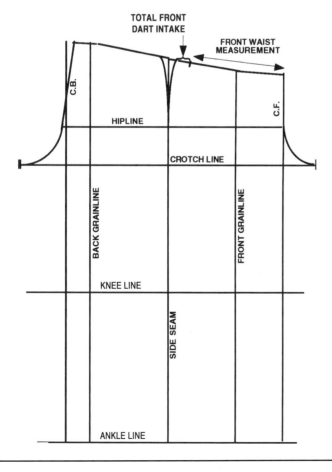

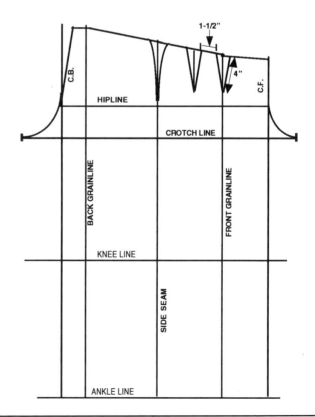

19 FIGURE THE BACK DART AMOUNTS

Measure from the center back toward the side seam using the back waist quarter measurement. Crossmark this position.

The distance between the new side seam and the crossmark is the total dart intake.
(For two darts, divide this amount in half.)

BACK DART(S) AMOUNT _____

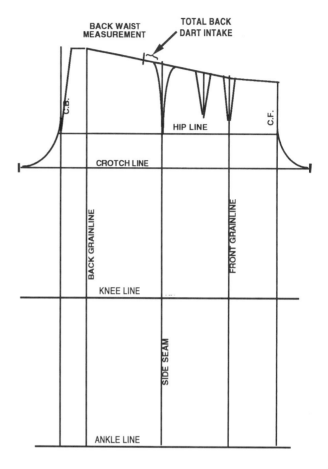

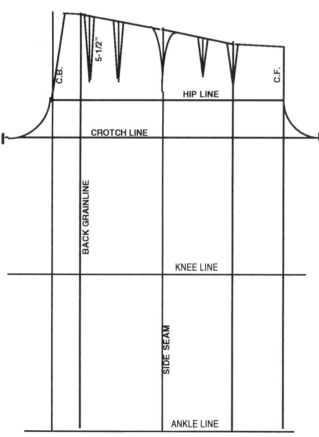

20 DRAW THE BACK WAISTLINE DARTS

A Place the first dart 1/4 inch from the back grainline. Crossmark the the width using the back dart amount.

B Place the second dart 1-1/2" (1-1/4" for smaller sizes) from the first dart and crossmark the back dart amount.

C Square and draw the center of each dart 5 inches long. Connect all points as illustrated.

NOTE: Back dart lengths may vary, depending on the design, but they should always be 1 inch longer than the front darts and never be longer than 6 inches.

PANT DRAFT FOR THE MATURE FIGURE

21 SELECT THE ANKLE WIDTH

Choose the hem width and divide the amount in half. Add 1/2 inch to this amount for the back width. Subtract 1/2 inch for the front width. (The front width should be 1 inch smaller than the back width.) Crossmark half of these measurement on each side of the grainline.

NOTE: A basic pant block for the mature figure uses an ankle width of 16 inches. (7-1/2 inches for the front and 8-1/2 inches for the back.) Crossmark half of these measurements on each side of the grainline.

- **3-3/4 inches on both sides of the FRONT GRAINLINE**
- **4-1/4 inches on both sides of the BACK GRAINLINE**

NOTE FOR SMALLER SIZES: 14" width for smaller sizes (see step #21 of the BASIC FITTED PANT for measurements)

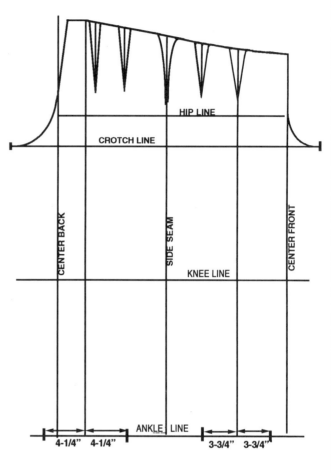

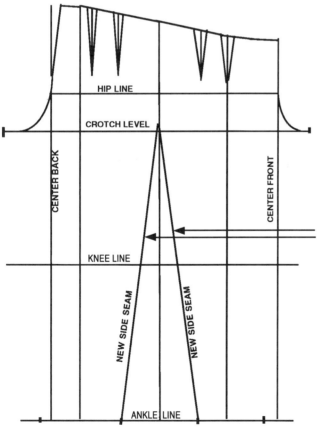

22 DRAW THE SIDE SEAM LEGGING

For both the Front and Back: Draw a new line from the ankle crossmark to the side seam at the crotch level. (These lines are new side seams.)

23 DRAW THE FRONT IN-SEAM LEGGING

A On the knee level, measure from the new front side seam to the front grain-line. Extend this same amount from the opposite side of the front grainline. Crossmark.

B Using a long ruler, connect the ankle crossmark to the knee level cross-mark and continue extending this line up to the crotch line.

C Using a hip curve ruler, blend the end of the front crotch line into the new inseam as illustrated.

24 DEVELOP THE BACK INSEAM LEGGING

A On the knee level, measure from the new back side seam to the back grain-line. Extend the same measurement from the opposite side of the back grainline. Crossmark.

B Using a long ruler, connect the ankle crossmark to the knee level crossmark and continue extending this line up to the crotch line.

C Using a hip curve ruler, blend the end of the back crotch line into the new inseam line as illustrated

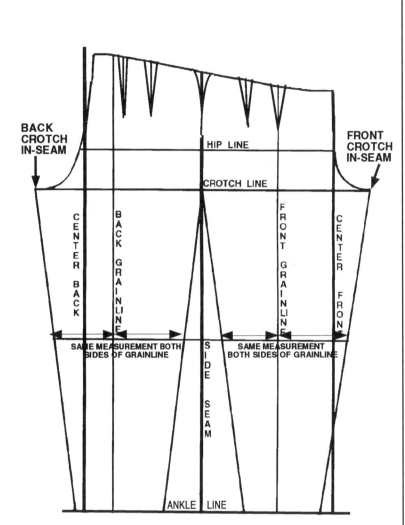

25 BALANCE THE FRONT AND BACK IN-SEAMS

A Pin the front and back to each other at the ankle in-seams and knee in-seams. (If the paper twists when these two positions are pinned to each other, an error was made during the drafting process or the pattern lines are not perfectly squared.)

B When the in-seams are pinned in place, note the position of the back crotch in-seam and the front crotch in-seam.PANT STYLING If these two positions do not match, divide the difference in half and make a new inseam crossmark.

C Using a hip-curve ruler, reblend a new in-seam from the crotch to the knee level. This makes the front and back in-seams the same shape and length.

NOTE: If the divided distance is more than 3/8 inch, an error was made in the measurement and/or drafting process.

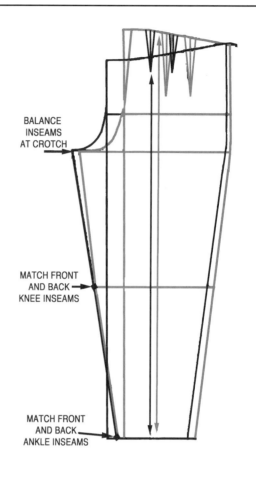

BALANCE INSEAMS AT CROTCH

MATCH FRONT AND BACK KNEE INSEAMS

MATCH FRONT AND BACK ANKLE INSEAMS

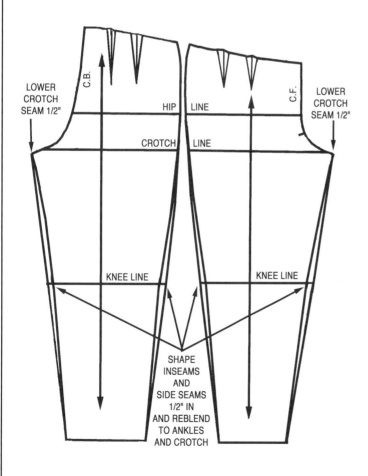

LOWER CROTCH SEAM 1/2"

C.B.

HIP LINE

CROTCH LINE

C.F.

LOWER CROTCH SEAM 1/2"

KNEE LINE

KNEE LINE

SHAPE INSEAMS AND SIDE SEAMS 1/2" IN AND REBLEND TO ANKLES AND CROTCH

26 SHAPE LEGGING AND CUT THE PATTERN OUT

A To prevent the "bagging" effect, shape the legging as illustrated. Refer to **FINAL FITTING PROCEDURES** of the Basic Fitted Pants to complete the fitting of the waistline and side seam.

B Add all appropriate seam allowances and cut the pattern out. Re-check the following areas:

- In-seam Balance – in-seams should be the **SAME SHAPE AND LENGTH** when the grainlines are parallel to each other.

- Side Seam Balance – side seams should be the **SAME SHAPE AND LENGTH** when the grainlines are parallel to each other.

- Mark all sewing notches.

PANT STYLING

The following pattern principles will teach you how to design various pant styles after the completion and fitting of the basic pant block. Learning these basic styles provides endless possibilities as you create with various colors and fabrics.

Legging width, fullness, and length will change with fashion seasons. However, the following styles are foundational silhouettes used for the majority of pant designs.

HIP YOKE DESIGNS

The hip yoke is a fitted section with a horizontal seam in the hip area. This yoke seam may be drawn parallel to the waistline, or shaped into any pointed or curved shape desired. A yoke can be designed in both the front and back of a pant, or in only one of these areas. To make a yoke design, a styline is drawn and cut, dividing the pant into two sections. On the yoke section, the original darts are slashed and closed, leaving a clean-fitteding yoke area. To complete the design, the yoke area may be faced or connected to a waistband.

HIP YOKE JEANS WITH TAPERED LEG

1 Trace the front and back pant block onto pattern paper. Draw in the darts.
NOTE: Seam allowances are already on the pant block.

2 Draw in the desired yoke styleline for both the front and back pant. Mark notches on the front and back styleline as illustrated.

3 Cut apart the pattern on the styleline.

4 Slash and close the darts in the yoke area.

5 Eliminate the remaining pant dart excess by removing that amount from the side seams and the centers.

6 Add seam allowances to the yoke and pant styleline.

TO COMPLETE THE JEAN FIT:
7 Raise the crotch UP 1/2 inch and IN 1/2 inch.

8 At the ankle, crossmark 1 inch IN on all four seams.

9 From the new crotch position, taper the legging to the new ankle crossmarks.

10 FINISH THE PATTERN:
- Choose a WAISTBAND style and width. (Refer to WAISTBAND pages for detailed instructions.)
- Design a BUTTON OR ZIPPER OPENING. (Refer to ZIPPER OPENINGS for detailed instructions.)
- Add any additional details such as pockets, patches, or trims.

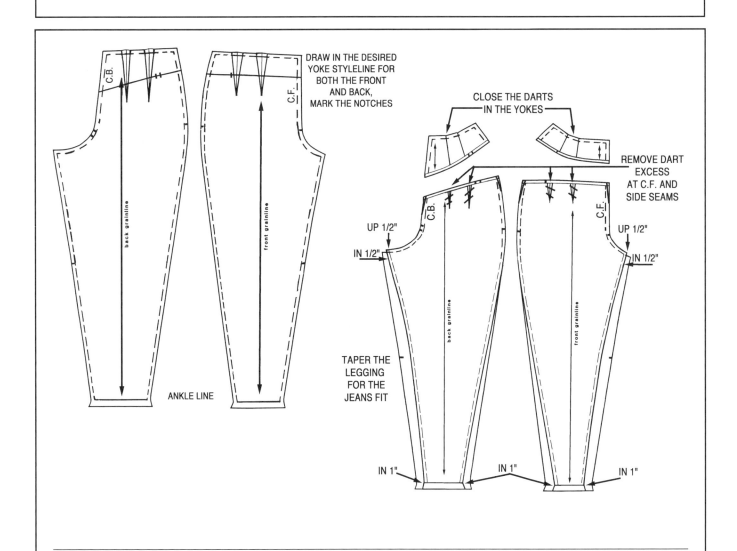

DRAW IN THE DESIRED YOKE STYLELINE FOR BOTH THE FRONT AND BACK, MARK THE NOTCHES

C.B.

C.F.

ANKLE LINE

CLOSE THE DARTS IN THE YOKES

REMOVE DART EXCESS AT C.F. AND SIDE SEAMS

UP 1/2"

IN 1/2"

C.B.

back grainline

TAPER THE LEGGING FOR THE JEANS FIT

IN 1"

IN 1"

UP 1/2"

IN 1/2"

C.F.

front grainline

IN 1"

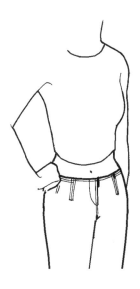

HIP HUGGER PANTS

A hip hugger pant design uses the same pattern process as a hip yoke design, except you do not use the yoke. To complete the waist edge of the Hip Hugger Design, refer to page 55, Faced Waistline.

PANTS WITH PLEATS AND TUCKs
TWO PLEAT – BUDGET

BUDGET-PLEATED Pants are created by using the existing front waist darts as pleats. The darts are unsewn and instead folded and pressed from notch to notch. A waistband is needed to hold the pressed pleats in place. The back design keeps the original darts, these are not converted into pleats.

1. Trace the pant blocks onto pattern paper. Erase the existing front darts, but leave the original notches that mark the dart width.
NOTE: Seam allowances are already on the pant blocks.

2. Convert the front darts into pleats by keeping the exiting notches. (These will be folded to each other during construction.)
NOTE: The back pant darts are not converted into pleats.

3. **FOR A CUFF:**
Choose the cuff width. Add this amount 3 times to the original ankle/hem-line. Fold the cuff and cut the pattern inseams and side seams following the shape of the legging.

4. **FINISH THE PATTERN:**
   - Choose a WAISTBAND style and width. (Refer to the WAISTBAND pages for detailed instructions.)
   - Design a BUTTON OR ZIPPER OPENING. (Refer to the ZIPPER OPENINGS pages for detailed instructions.)
   - Add any additional details such as pockets, patches or trims.

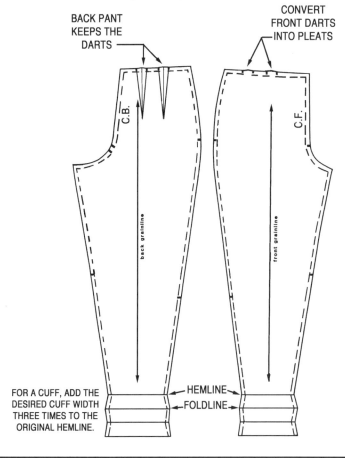

BACK PANT KEEPS THE DARTS

CONVERT FRONT DARTS INTO PLEATS

C.B.

C.F.

back grainline

front grainline

FOR A CUFF, ADD THE DESIRED CUFF WIDTH THREE TIMES TO THE ORIGINAL HEMLINE.

HEMLINE
FOLDLINE

PANTS WITH PLEATS AND TUCKS
TWO PLEAT – FULL

Full Two-Pleat pants are created by slashing the pattern and adding fullness in the waist area. Each pleat is positioned on the original dart areas. During construction, the pleats are folded and pressed from notch to notch. A waistband is needed to hold the pressed pleats into place. The back pant keeps the original darts, these are not converted into pleats.

1   Trace the pant blocks onto pattern paper. Erase the front darts.

2   Slash and open the front pant grainline to the desired width of the first pleat.

3   The second pleat uses the amount of both original darts. Place this amount where the second pleat is desired.
    NOTE: The back pant darts and are not converted into pleats.

4   **FINISH THE PATTERN:**
    ▪ Choose a WAISTBAND style and width. (Refer to the WAISTBAND pages for detailed instructions.)
    ▪ Design a BUTTON OR ZIPPER OPENING. (Refer to the ZIPPER OPENINGS pages for detailed instructions.)
    ▪ Add any additional details such as pockets, patches or trims.

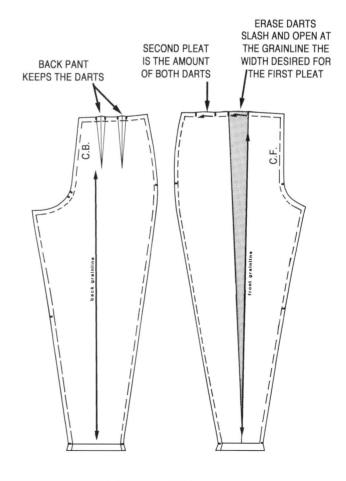

BACK PANT
KEEPS THE DARTS

SECOND PLEAT
IS THE AMOUNT
OF BOTH DARTS

ERASE DARTS
SLASH AND OPEN AT
THE GRAINLINE THE
WIDTH DESIRED FOR
THE FIRST PLEAT

C.B.

C.F.

back grainline

front grainline

PANTS WITH PLEATS AND TUCKS
THREE PLEAT PANTS

Pants with three front waistline pleats are created by slashing the pattern and adding fullness in the waist area. Two pleats are positioned where the original darts were placed. The third pleat is usually placed halfway between center front and the first pleat. During construction, these pleats are folded and pressed from notch to notch. A waistband is needed to hold the pressed pleats in place. The back pant darts are not converted into pleats.

1. Trace the pant blocks onto pattern paper.
2. For the pleat closest to center front, slash the front pattern halfway between center front and the first dart. Open this area to the amount desired for the pleat.
3. Slash and open the middle of the existing front darts until they equal the width of the first pleat (measure from original notch to notch).
   NOTE: The back pant darts are not converted into pleats.

4. **FINISH THE PATTERN:**
   - Choose a WAISTBAND style and width. (Refer to the WAISTBAND pages for detailed instructions.)
   - Design a BUTTON OR ZIPPER OPENING. (Refer to the ZIPPER OPENINGS pages for detailed instructions.)
   - Add any additional details such as pockets, patches or trims.

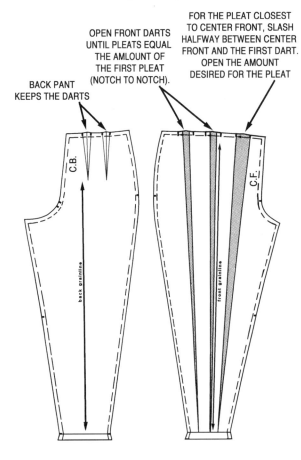

BACK PANT KEEPS THE DARTS

OPEN FRONT DARTS UNTIL PLEATS EQUAL THE AMLOUNT OF THE FIRST PLEAT (NOTCH TO NOTCH).

FOR THE PLEAT CLOSEST TO CENTER FRONT, SLASH HALFWAY BETWEEN CENTER FRONT AND THE FIRST DART. OPEN THE AMOUNT DESIRED FOR THE PLEAT

C.B.

C.F.

back grainline

front grainline

PANTS WITH PLEATS AND TUCKS
RELEASE TUCKS WITH STRAIGHT LEGS

Front waistline tucks are created by slashing the pattern and adding fullness in the waist area. A tuck is usually sewn to 2 inches down from the waistline. This releases into a bit of fullness at the lower end of the tuck. No fullness is added to the back waistline, therefore, the back darts are not converted into tucks.

1 Slash and open the middle of each dart to the desired width of the tucks. (The desired width of the tuck is determined by the amount opened plus the original dart size – notch to notch).

2 Draw the width of the tucks as illustrated. Draw the bottom of the tucks at the length desired. (This creats the stitchlines of the tucks).

3 Add seam allowances to the stitchline of the tucks as pictured.

4 For a straight legging, taper the legging as illustrated.

5 **FINISH THE PATTERN:**
   - Choose a WAISTBAND style and width. (Refer to the WAISTBAND pages for detailed instructions.)
   - Design a BUTTON OR ZIPPER OPENING. (Refer to the ZIPPER OPEN-INGS pages for detailed instructions.)
   - Add any additional details such as pockets, patches or trims.

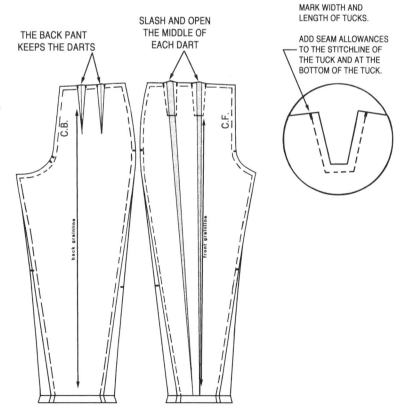

THE BACK PANT KEEPS THE DARTS

SLASH AND OPEN THE MIDDLE OF EACH DART

MARK WIDTH AND LENGTH OF TUCKS.

ADD SEAM ALLOWANCES TO THE STITCHLINE OF THE TUCK AND AT THE BOTTOM OF THE TUCK.

PANTS WITH GATHERED WAIST

A gathered waist design creates extra fullness in the pant waistline by squaring the side seams and leaving the darts unsewn. The fullness in the waistline is gathered and sewn to a separate straight waistband. This waist style is recommended for plus-size women because of their pattern's waistline slope.

1   Trace the blocks onto pattern paper. Erase the front and back original darts. The dart area will become part of the gathered fullness.

2   Square up the side seams from the hipline.

3   **COMPLETE THE PATTERN DESIGN**
    - Choose a WAISTBAND style and width. (Refer to the WAISTBAND pages for detailed instructions.)
    - Design a BUTTON OR ZIPPER OPENING. (Refer to the ZIPPER OPENINGS pages for detailed instructions.)
    - Add any additional details such as pockets, patches or trims.

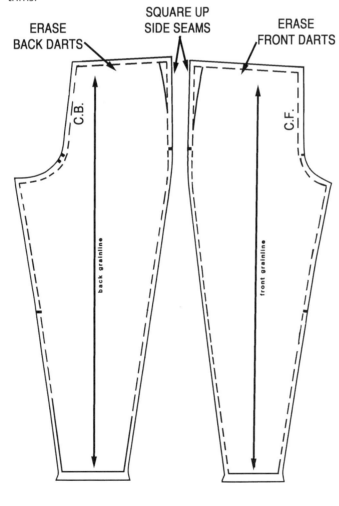

ERASE BACK DARTS

SQUARE UP SIDE SEAMS

ERASE FRONT DARTS

C.B.

C.F.

back grainline

front grainline

PANTS WITH GATHERED ELASTIC WAIST

Gathered elastic waist designs create extra fullness in the pant waistline by squaring the side seams and leaving the darts unsewn. An extension is added to the pattern waistline that is double the width of a waistband. When sewn, this extension creates a waistband casing through which an elastic strip is pulled. This allows the pants to be pulled on over the hips, eliminating the need for a zipper opening.

1   Trace the blocks onto pattern paper. Erase the front and back darts. This area will become part of the gathered fullness.

2   **S**quare the side seams and center back up from the hipline.

3   On the waistline, add the desired waistband width. (usually 1-1/2 inches or 2 inches).

4   Add this same amount again plus 1/4 inch.

5   Notch the foldline as illustrated.

ELASTIC LENGTH: The elastic should be cut the length of the waist measurement minus 1 inch.

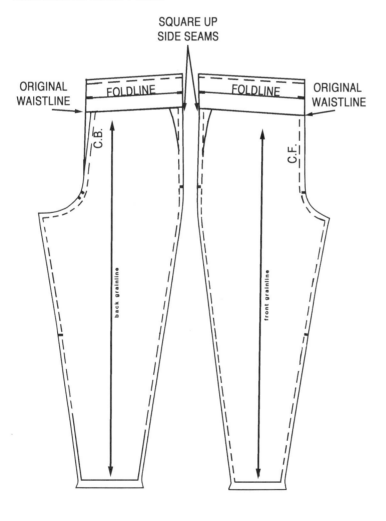

FATIGUE PANTS/BLOUSED PANT/HAREM PANTS

Fatigue, Bloused, and Harem are different names for the same basic pant style. These styles add fullness at the pant waistline and ankle. The fullness added to the ankle varies, depending upon the design. The pant hem is gathered to a band, or an elastic casing is made for inserting elastic.

1   Trace the blocks onto pattern paper. Erase the front and back original darts. This area will become part of the gathered fullness.

2   Square the side seams straight up from the hipline.

3   To create the legging fullness, extend the side seams and inseams straight down from the crotch level.

4   **COMPLETE THE PATTERN DESIGN:**
    - Choose a WAISTBAND style and width. (Refer to the WAISTBAND pages for detailed instructions.)
    - Design a BUTTON OR ZIPPER OPENING. (Refer to the ZIPPER OPENINGS pages for detailed instructions.)
    - Add any additional details such as pockets, patches or trims.

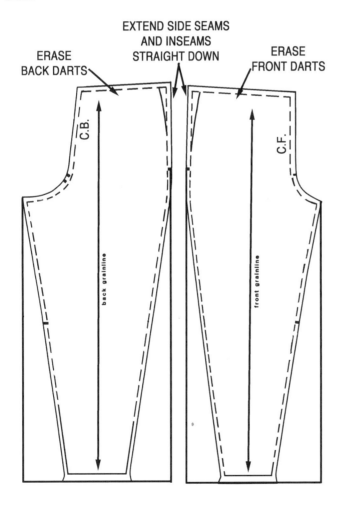

ERASE
BACK DARTS

EXTEND SIDE SEAMS
AND INSEAMS
STRAIGHT DOWN

ERASE
FRONT DARTS

C.B.

back grainline

C.F.

front grainline

PALAZZO PANTS

Palazzo pants are characterized by the wide, sweeping leg opening at the hem level. This style is created by *slashing* and *opening* the pattern legging. The amount of fullness added depends on the desired style and the fabric being used.

1   Trace the blocks onto pattern paper. Square the side seams and the inseams down from the crotch level to create part of the legging fullness.

2   Slash the legging from the hemline up to the waistline, and open the pattern to the desired fullness.

3   Convert the front and back darts into pleats by keeping the existing notches and erasing the dart points.
    NOTE: Sometimes the back darts are not converted into pleats.

4   COMPLETE THE PATTERN DESIGN
    ▪ Choose a WAISTBAND style and width. (Refer to the WAISTBAND pages for detailed instructions.)
    ▪ Design a BUTTON OR ZIPPER OPENING. (Refer to the ZIPPER OPENINGS pages for detailed instructions.)
    ▪ Add any additional details such as pockets, patches or trims.

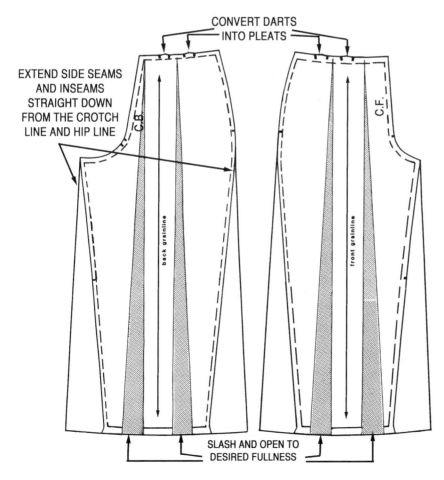

PANTS WITH HIGH WAIST

Pants with a high waist are designed with a raised fitted waist area, similar to a midriff design. The raised portion may be added as an extension to the pattern or cut as a separate panel and sewn to the waist seam of the pants. The snug-to-the-body fit is created with shaped side seams and fisheye darts.

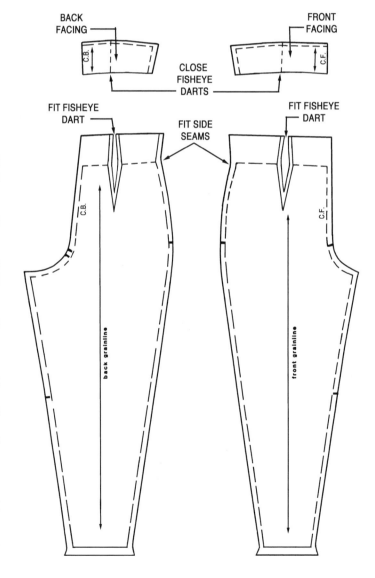

1 Trace the blocks onto pattern paper. Extend center front and center back straight up to the desired design height.

2 Extend both side seams up and out from the waistline to the desired height.

3 Place pants on model. Drape in one fisheye dart and shape the side seams to the desired fit.

4 Add seam allowances around each fisheye dart to create a cut-away dart. (see example)

5 Make front and back facings:
   A Trace the raised waist area of both the front and back pant.
   B Make facings 2-1/2 inches wide from the top edge of the traced area.
   C Slash and close the fisheye dart area on both facing pieces.

6 **COMPLETE THE PATTERN DESIGN**
   ▪ Design a BUTTON OR ZIPPER OPENING. (Refer to the ZIPPER OPENINGS pages for detailed instructions.)
   ▪ Add any additional details such as pockets, patches or trims.

VARIOUS PANT LENGTH STYLES

Each pant may be designed at any length desired. Changing the pant length easily creates an entirely different look. Many lengths have traditional names. The following picture illustrates the most common lengths and their style names.

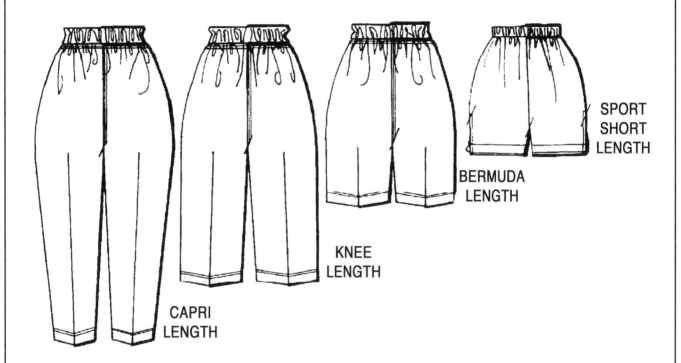

FIGURING THE PANT LENGTH

1 Choose your design length.

2 Measure from the waistline (at the side seam) to the length desired. Transfer this measurement to the pattern.

SHORT CROPPED PANTS (CAPRI-PEDAL PUSHERS)

Short cropped pants may also be referred to as Capris or Pedal Pushers (which were popular during the 1950's). This is a three-quarter length pant with a short slit on the outside of each legging. The pattern example illustrates a common length. However, you may make the pattern at any length.

1 Raise the hem level to the desired design length.

2 Taper the legging to the desired width. Reduce the seams equally on all four sides.

3 Mark slit notch on side seams.

4 **COMPLETE THE PATTERN DESIGN**
  ▪ Add new seam/hem allowance.
  ▪ Choose a WAISTBAND style and width. (Refer to the WAISTBAND pages for detailed instructions.)
  ▪ Design a BUTTON OR ZIPPER OPENING. (Refer to the ZIPPER OPENINGS pages for detailed instructions.)
  ▪ Add any additional details such as pockets, patches or trims.

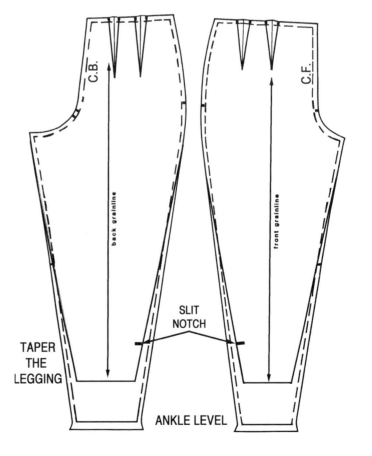

WALKING SHORTS WITH A CUFF

Walking shorts finish just above the knee. This style can be worn as sport shorts or matched with a jacket. The pattern example illustrates a common length for a walking short. However, you may make the pattern at any length.

1   Trace the blocks onto pattern paper. Erase the existing front darts.

2   Convert the front darts into pleats by keeping the original width notches. NOTE: The back darts are not converted into pleats.

3   Mark a new hemline. Draw it square with the grainline.

4   For a cuff, choose the cuff width. Add this amount three times to the hemline. Fold the cuff and cut the pattern inseam and side seam following the shape of the legging.

5   **COMPLETE THE PATTERN DESIGN**
- Choose a WAISTBAND style and width. (Refer to the WAISTBAND pages for detailed instructions.)
- Design a BUTTON OR ZIPPER OPENING. (Refer to the ZIPPER OPENINGS pages for detailed instructions.)
- Add any additional details such as pockets, patches or trims.

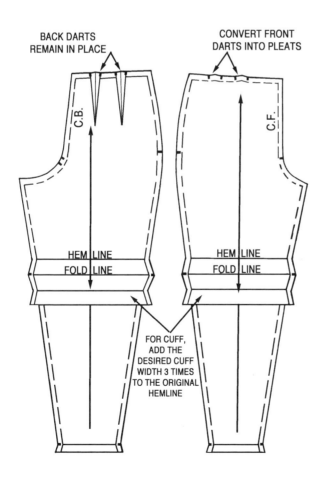

BACK DARTS REMAIN IN PLACE

CONVERT FRONT DARTS INTO PLEATS

C.B.

C.F.

HEM LINE
FOLD LINE

HEM LINE
FOLD LINE

FOR CUFF, ADD THE DESIRED CUFF WIDTH 3 TIMES TO THE ORIGINAL HEMLINE

SPORT SHORTS

Sports shorts are usually worn as exercise shorts, running shorts, or track shorts and typically feature a pull-on elastic waist.

1   Trace the pant blocks onto pattern paper. Erase the front and back darts. This area becomes part of the gathered (elastic) fullness.

2   Square the front and back side seams straight up from the hipline.

3   At the waistline, add the desired width of the waist elastic casing (usually 1-1/2 inches or 2 inches.) Add this same amount again plus 1/4 inch.

4   Notch the foldlines as illustrated.
    NOTE: The elastic length should stretch to the hip measurement, plus 1 inch for overlapping.

5   Lower the crotch DOWN 1/4 inch and crossmark. Bring the crotch IN 1/4 inch

6   Reshape a new front and back crotch.

7   Mark the desired legging length on both side seams and inseams.
    A Crossmark the INSEAMS IN 1 INCH.
    B Crossmark the SIDE SEAMS IN 1/2 inch.
    C Reshape new inseams and side seams.

8   Add a 1 inch hem. Also, fold up the hem amount and shape the hem area following the new side seams and inseams.

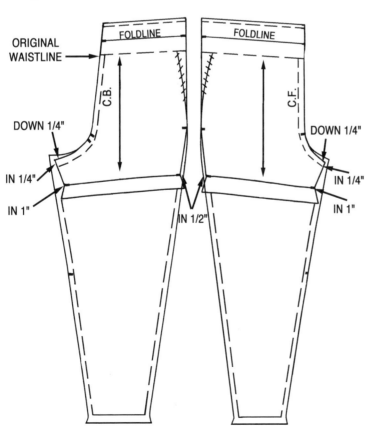

SPORT CULOTTES/TWO PLEAT (BUDGET)

Sport culottes are a pant designed to look like a skirt and drape similar to a split skirt. A pleat hides the front crotch seam, resulting in a skirt look with all the comforts of a pair of pants.

1   Trace the pant blocks onto pattern paper. Optional: Convert the front darts into pleats by erasing the front darts and leaving the original width notches.

2   Draw a new hemline squared with the grainline.

3   Cut open the pattern on center front. Add 5 inches at center front for the legging pleat (see illustration). NOTE: The back pant legging does not have a pleat.

4   Square down the side seams and the inseams on both the front and back pant.

5   For additional crotch ease, extend the front and back crotch out 1/2 inch.

6   **COMPLETE THE PATTERN DESIGN**
    - Choose a WAISTBAND style and width. (Refer to the WAIST-BAND pages for detailed instructions.)
    - Design a BUTTON OR ZIPPER OPENING. (Refer to the ZIPPER OPENINGS pages for detailed instructions.)
    - Add any addiHtional details such as pockets, patches or trims.

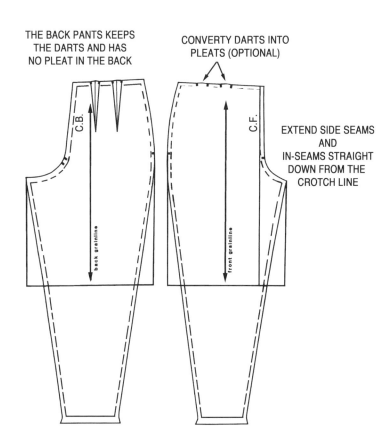

THE BACK PANTS KEEPS
THE DARTS AND HAS
NO PLEAT IN THE BACK

CONVERTY DARTS INTO
PLEATS (OPTIONAL)

C.B.

C.F.

back grainline

front grainline

EXTEND SIDE SEAMS
AND
IN-SEAMS STRAIGHT
DOWN FROM THE
CROTCH LINE

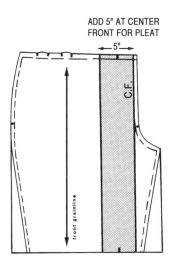

ADD 5" AT CENTER
FRONT FOR PLEAT

5"

C.F.

front grainline

TRADITIONAL JUMPSUIT

A traditional jumpsuit is a darted bodice and pant combined in one piece with a zipper or button front opening. It is worn for sports and leisure wear by both men and women. When using this block, the design must include a position for the shoulder dart. It may be trasfered to another dart location or turned into shirring, tucks, or stylelines. The waistline fisheye darts are optional, depending upon the desired style and fit of the design.

1   Trace the pants blocks onto pattern paper. Square the center front line up past the waist-line.

2   Add 1/2 inch at center back and crossmark. Square and draw in a new center back line up past the waistline.

3   Square both front and back side seams up from the hip level.

4   Erase the original pant waistline darts.

5   Align the TORSO block to the pant block:
    A Align the center front waist position of the torso block 1/2 inch above the center front waist position of the pant.
    B Align the center back waist position of the torso block 1/2 inch above the center back waist position of the pant
    C The waistlines at the side seams will auto-matically match.
    D Trace the torso block, including all darts.

6   From this traditional jumpsuit block, continue to develop the remainder of the design.

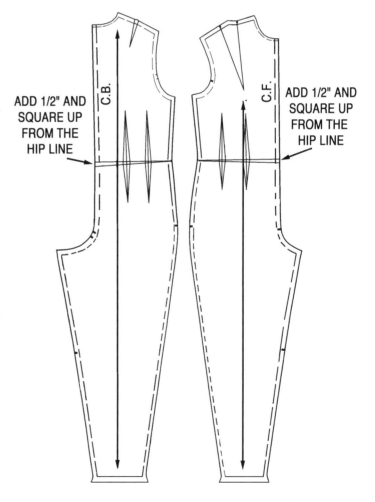

ADD 1/2" AND SQUARE UP FROM THE HIP LINE

C.B.

C.F.

ADD 1/2" AND SQUARE UP FROM THE HIP LINE

SAFARI JUMPSUIT

A safari jumpsuit is a dartless shirt and trouser combined in one piece and zipped or buttoned up the front. It is worn for sports and leisure wear by both men and women. When made in a knit fabric, it is referred to as a body suit. A playsuit is a shortened version of this block.

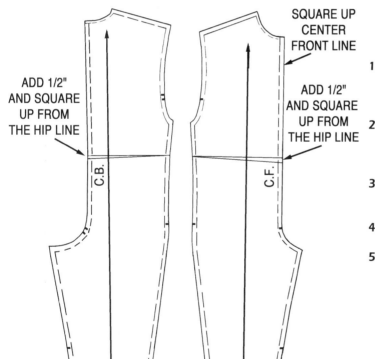

ADD 1/2"
AND SQUARE
UP FROM
THE HIP LINE

C.B.

SQUARE UP
CENTER
FRONT LINE

ADD 1/2"
AND SQUARE
UP FROM
THE HIP LINE

C.F.

1 Trace the pant blocks onto pattern paper. Square the center front line up past the waistline.

2 Add 1/2 inch at center back and crossmark. Square and draw in a new center back line up past the waistline.

3 Square both front and back side seams up from the hip level.

4 Erase the original pant waistline darts.

5 Align the TORSO block to the pant block:
  A Align the center front waist position of the torso block 1/2 inch above the center front waist position of the pant.
  B Align the center back waist position of the torso block 1/2 inch above the center back waist position of the pant
  C The waistlines at the side seams will automatically match.
  D Trace the torso block, including all darts.

6 From this safari jumpsuit block, continue to develop the remainder of the design.

FASHION OVERALLS

Overalls are pants with a bib top and suspender straps that cross in the back and attach over the shoulders. Traditionally worn by farmers, house painters railroad workers, and carpenters, in today's fashion they are designed for all genders and ages. These popular pants are created in an assortment of fabrics and designed with a variety of pockets and bib styles.

FROM THIS JUMPSUIT BLOCK, CONTINUE TO DEVELP THE PATTERN FOR THE FASHION OVERALLS

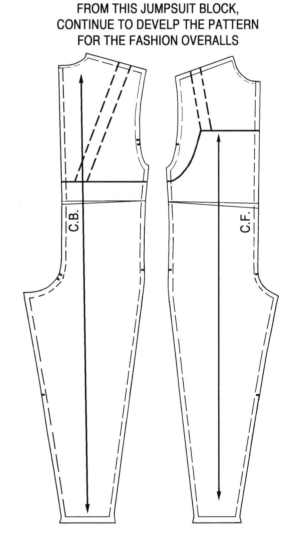

1 Trace the safari jumpsuit block onto new pattern paper.

2 Draw in the desired bib styleline (new neckline, new armholes) and any pocket locations.

3 Make the appropriate facings and strappings.

WAISTLINE TREATMENTS

Waistline Treatments finish the top portion of pants and secure it to the body. These treatments may also include button or hook closures, drawsting closures, and various creative design closures. A pant waistline may be joined to a Traditional Fitted Waistband (which is sewn to the waist seam of the pants) or be finished with a facing. A common casual and sport waistline treatment is an elastic casing, which is an extension added to the waistline of the pant pattern.

TRADITIONAL FITTED WAISTBAND

The TRADITIONAL FITTED WAISTBAND is a separate straight band of fabric that fits the waist measurement and includes an extension for button or hook closures. This band is usually interfaced and then stitched to the waistline of the pants. The waistband extends upwards from the actual pant waistline and is fastened firmly around the waistline.

FIGURING THE WAISTBAND NOTCHES

1   On a scrap strip of paper, mark one-half of the waistline measurement used to develop the waistline of the pant. Note the right mark as C.F. and the left mark as C.B.

2   Fold the paper in half, matching the marks.

3   **U**nfold the paper and crossmark the quarter fold 1/4 inch toward the center back. (This makes the front waist measurement 1/2 inch larger than the back waist measurement.) MEASURE THE DISTANCES BETWEEN THE MARKS AND USE THEM IN THE DRAFT BELOW.

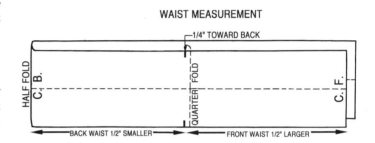

WAIST MEASUREMENT

DRAFTING THE WAISTBAND

1   Fold a piece of paper in half lengthwise.

2   Measure from the fold using 1/2 the waistline measurement (including the 1 inch of ease). Crossmark and square a line (this is the C.F. line).

3   Draw the waistband twice the desired finished width. (Usually 1-1/2 inches finished, 3 inches total pattern width.)

4   Using the waist quarter measurements figured above, place notches at center front, side seams, and center back.

5   Add seam allowances to all seams.

6   Add 1 inch extra to one center front end for the button/hook extension amount.
NOTE: If the pant is designed with a back opening, add the extension to the center back line. Match and tape the C.F. lines together.

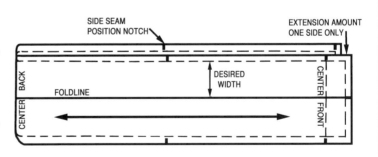

WAISTBAND VARIATIONS

The following waisband variations differ only in where the waistband opens. To draft waistbands for CENTER BACK OPENING, LEFT SIDE SEAM OPENING, and WRAP AROUND OPENING, follow the draft for the traditional waistband with the following exceptions. Also, follow the INTERFAICNG THE WAIST-BAND instructions to draft the interfacing pattern.

DRAFTING THE CENTER BACK OPENING WAISTBAND
The paper fold is center front. The crossmarked waist length is center back. The button extension is added to only one center back line.

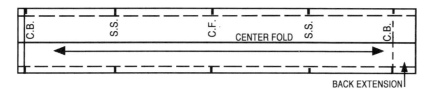

DRAFTING THE LEFT SIDE OPENING WAISTBAND
The paper fold is the right side seam. Measure away from both sides of the right seam using the Front and Back quarter waist measurements. The ends of these marks are the left side seams. Fold the left side seam to the right side seam to find the center front and center back positions.

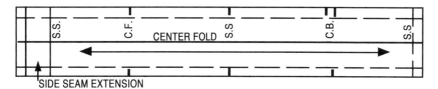

DRAFTING THE WRAP AROUND WAISTBAND
Begin marking and measuring in the same manner as a center front opening. Instead of adding a 1 inch extension onto the waistband, add the amount of the wrap extension to the center fronts.

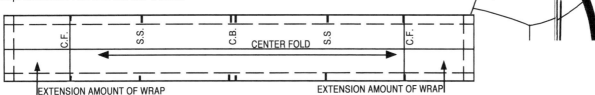

INTERFACING THE WAISTBAND
All waistbands should be interfaced to maintain shape and add durability. The entire waistband is not interfaced, the interfacing should only extend 1/2 inch beyond the center foldline of the waistband. After finishing the waistband pattern, make another copy. Draw a line 1/2 inch past the center foldline and draw lines 1/8 inch in from the outer pattern edges. Cut the Interfacing pattern on these new lines.

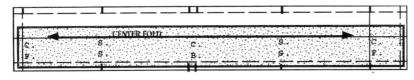

ELASTIC WAISTBAND & DRAWSTRING WAISTBAND

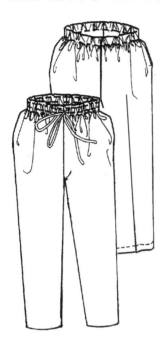

The ELASTIC WAISTBAND and the DRAWSTRING WAISTBAND are the same pattern draft. They both add an amount to the pant pattern waistline that is double the desired waistband width.

During the elastic waistband construction, the waistband is folded and stitched to creat a casing for elastic insertion. Or the fabric is shirred to the elastic with two or more rows of stitching and then folded and stitched.

The drawstring waistband is constructed by folding the waistband and stitching two rows in the center of the waist casing. Cording or ribbon is then inserted between the double row of stitching.

1   On the pant pattern, erase the waistline darts. These will become part of the waistline fullnes.

2   Draw a straight waistline from the side seams to center front and center back.

3   Square the side seams up from the hip line to create additional fullness that allows the pant to be pulled on over the hips.

4   Extend the center front and center back lines straight up.

5   On the waistline, add the desired width of the waistband (usually 1-1/2 inches or 2 inches).

6   Add this same amount again, plus 1/4 inch.

7   Notch the foldline (middle line).

MEASURE THE ELASTIC: The amount of elastic used should equal the waist measurement, minus 1 inch.

MEASURE THE CORDING: The amount of cording used should equal the waist measurement, plus 30 inches.

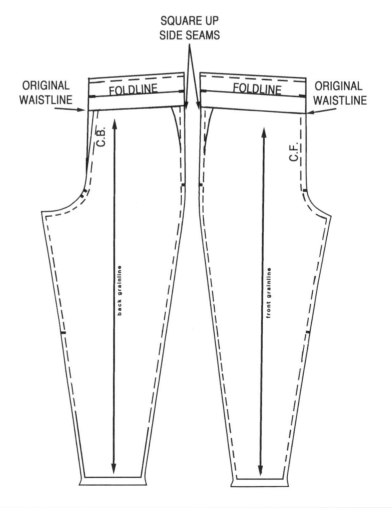

FACED WAISTLINE

A FACED WAISTLINE utilizes a separate 2-1/2 inch wide self-fabric piece. This shaped piece is stitched to the raw edge of the pant waistline, turned to the inside of the garment, lays flat, and finishes the waist edge. The garment waistline then rests at the body's natural waistline.

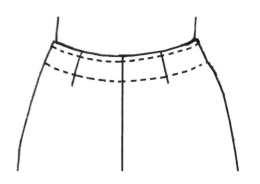

1   Trace the front and back waist area of the pant pattern.

2   Draw the facing 2-1/2 inches wide from the top edge of the traced pant.

3   Cut and close the waistline darts on both facing pieces.

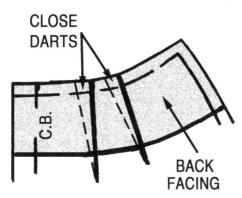

CLOSE DARTS

C.B.

BACK FACING

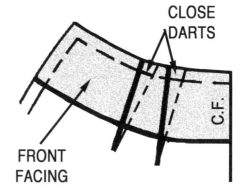

CLOSE DARTS

C.F.

FRONT FACING

SEWING DETAILS:
The side seam of the front and back waist facings are sewn to each other. The waistline of the facing is then placed to the correct side of the of the pant waist seam and stitched.

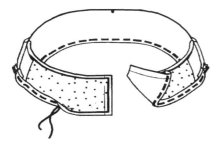

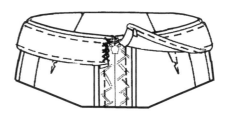

POCKET DESIGNS

POCKET DEFINITIONS

To assist novice patternmakers, we have included full-size copies of these pocket patterns on the following pages.

POCKET DESCRIPTIONS

Pockets are defined as shaped pieces of fabric sewn to the outside of a garment or set into a garment seam or opening. Used as decorative details that can carry small articles, e.g., handkerchiefs or coins, pockets can be functional designs or simply decorative designs.

POCKET DESIGNS

Pockets can be designed in a variety of sizes and shapes. They can be applied to the outside of the garment or sewn into the garment itself, such as a welt or buttonhole pocket. There are four basic types of pockets.

- The **Patch Pocket** is stitched to the surface of the garment. It can have rounded or squared corners at the base. A "patched" flap for the pocket can be designed in the same way. Patch pockets can be styled into skirts, pants, blouses, shirts, jackets or coats.

- The **Inseam Pocket** is neatly sewn into the side seam or styled seam of a garment and is usually made from matching fabric. It cannot be seen when the garment is worn.

- The **Front Hip Pocket** is an angled or curved pocket designed on the front of pants and skirts. They attach into the waist and side seam of the garment.

- The inside **Set-in Pocket (Bound)** is sewn into a slashed opening on a garment and is usually made with a single or double welt, and with or without a pocket flap. It is usually referred to as a "bound" pocket. Set-in variations only differ in the style of the welts and/or flaps that are sewn into the slashed opening. The four most common "bound" pockets are:
  – The Welt Bound Pocket
  – The One Piece Buttonhole Pocket
  – The Lined Buttonhole Pocket
  – The Bound Flap Pocket

SIDE SEAM POCKET

SIDE SEAM POCKET
This is the side seam pocket pattern.
Use this pattern in the side seam of
pants, skirts, and dresses.

DESCRIPTION
A side seam pocket is sewn
into a side seam and cannot
be seen when the garment
is worn.

SIDE SEAM POCKET

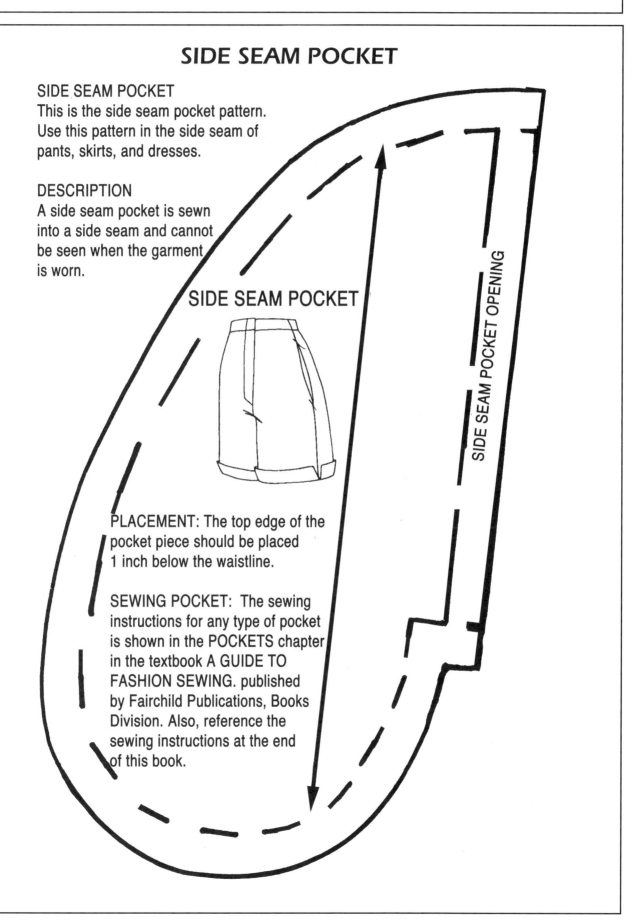

SIDE SEAM POCKET OPENING

PLACEMENT: The top edge of the
pocket piece should be placed
1 inch below the waistline.

SEWING POCKET: The sewing
instructions for any type of pocket
is shown in the POCKETS chapter
in the textbook A GUIDE TO
FASHION SEWING. published
by Fairchild Publications, Books
Division. Also, reference the
sewing instructions at the end
of this book.

FRONT HIP POCKET

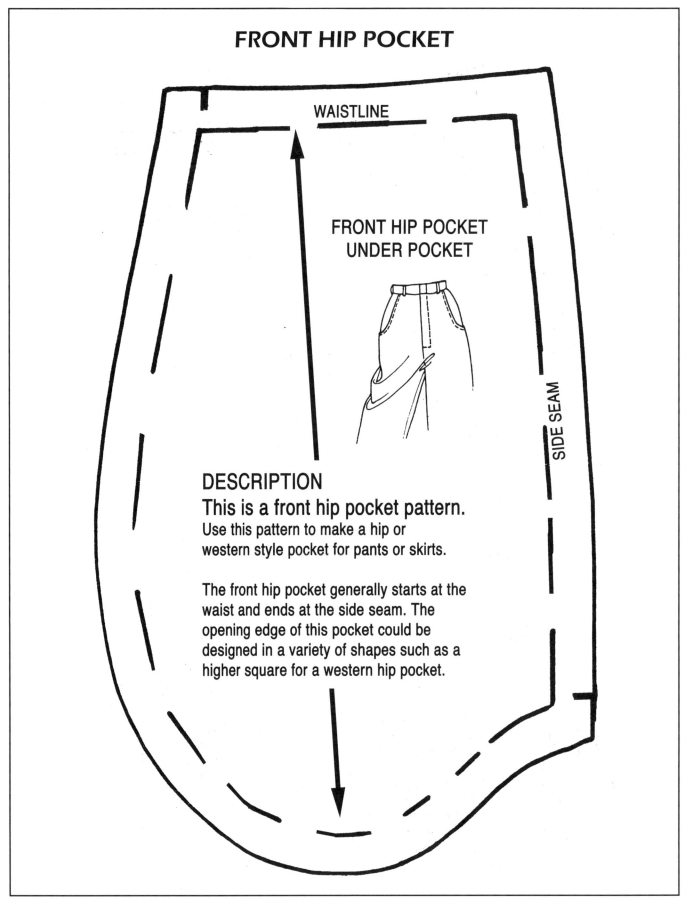

WAISTLINE

FRONT HIP POCKET
UNDER POCKET

SIDE SEAM

DESCRIPTION
This is a front hip pocket pattern.
Use this pattern to make a hip or
western style pocket for pants or skirts.

The front hip pocket generally starts at the
waist and ends at the side seam. The
opening edge of this pocket could be
designed in a variety of shapes such as a
higher square for a western hip pocket.

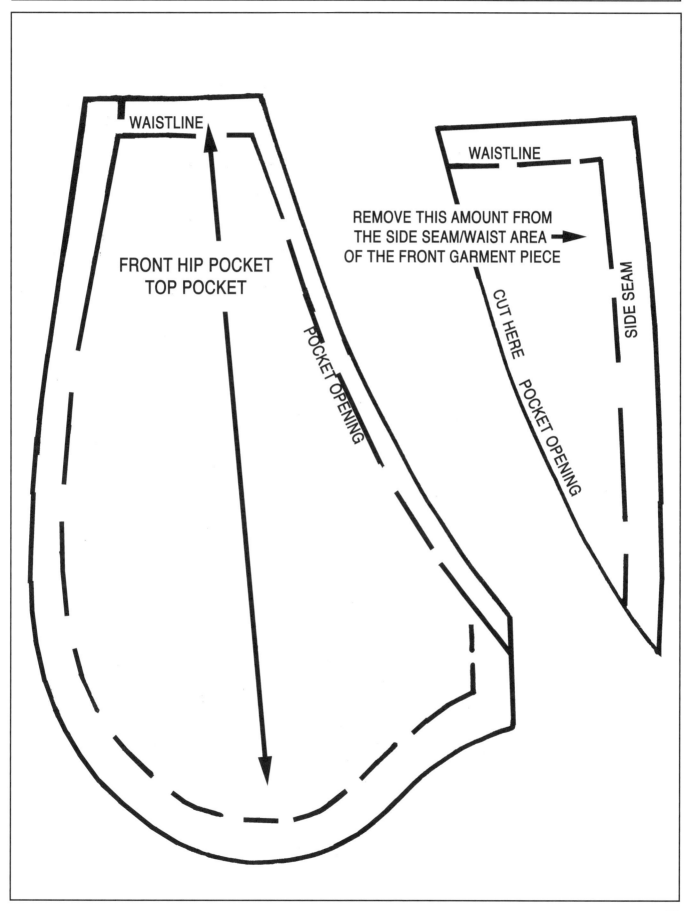

WAISTLINE

FRONT HIP POCKET
TOP POCKET

POCKET OPENING

WAISTLINE

REMOVE THIS AMOUNT FROM
THE SIDE SEAM/WAIST AREA →
OF THE FRONT GARMENT PIECE

SIDE SEAM

CUT HERE   POCKET OPENING

BUTTON & ZIPPER OPENINGS

To assist novice patternmakers, we have included full-size copies of zipper placket patterns on the following pages.

PANT OPENINGS provide access for opening and closing a pant style. Several types and lengths of zipper and button closures exist, and a variety of sewing techniques can be used with each one. The type selected for a garment design depends upon the design location of the zipper, and the type of fabric used in the garment.

BUTTON OPENINGS

Button openings can be a design effect or a practical opening for getting in and out of the pant. They may be placed at center front, center back, partially to the side, or on the side seam. Button openings require the same placket pieces as a traditional zipper placket. The buttons and buttonholes are placed after the placket pieces are sewn to the pant opening.

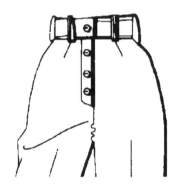

ZIPPER OPENINGS

Zippers openings are styled from the waistline down toward the crotch curve. They must be at least 7 to 9 inches long to allow for easy access in a pant. There are four basic zipper styles that can be easily sewn into a pant opening.

- The MOCK FLY-FRONT ZIPPER opening is most often used as a center front closing for pants. This is a less complicated method of inserting a fly-front zipper.

- The TRADITIONAL FLY-FRONT ZIPPER opening is a more tailored detail used in both women's and men's pants. Two placket pieces are sewn to the center front seam, one of which shields the zipper teeth from the body.

- The LAPPED ZIPPER opening conceals the zipper under a fold of the fabric. Only one row of stitching is visible on the correct side of the garment.

- The RAILROAD OR CENTERED ZIPPER opening has stitching visible on both sides of the zipper that is an equal distance from the center.

railroad zipper

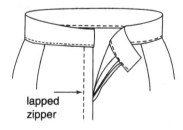

lapped zipper

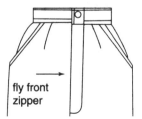

fly front zipper

TRADITIONAL FLY FRONT ZIPPER

The fly-front application is a more tailored detail used in both women's and men's pants.

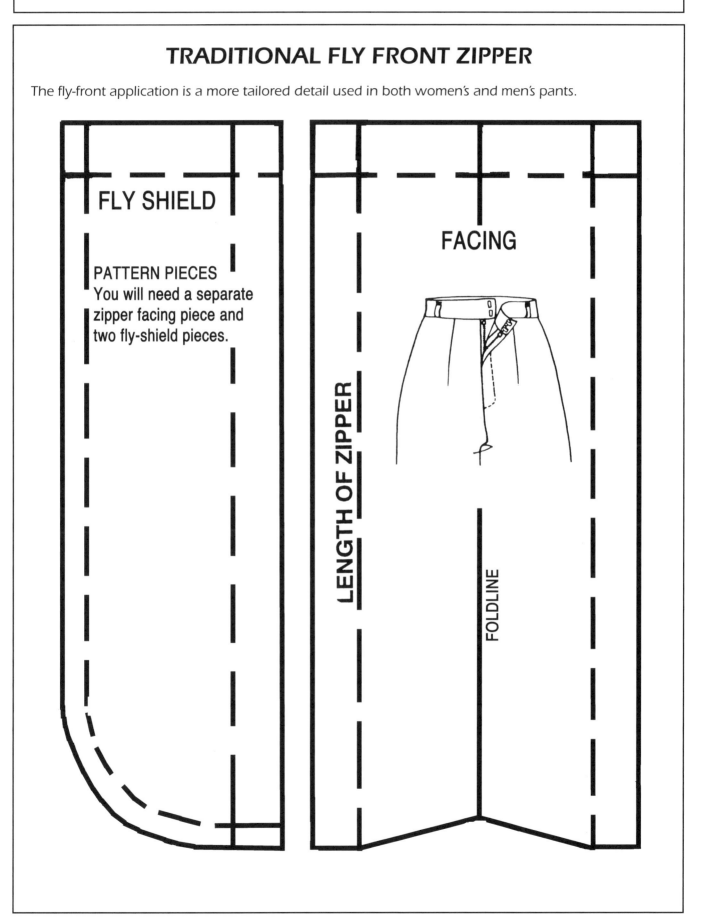

FLY SHIELD

PATTERN PIECES
You will need a separate zipper facing piece and two fly-shield pieces.

FACING

LENGTH OF ZIPPER

FOLDLINE

MOCK FLY FRONT ZIPPER

The mock fly-front zippler application is a simplified method of inserting a front pant zipper opening. This method is usually used only in women's pants. As illustrated here, an extension piece must be added to the front of the pants pattern.

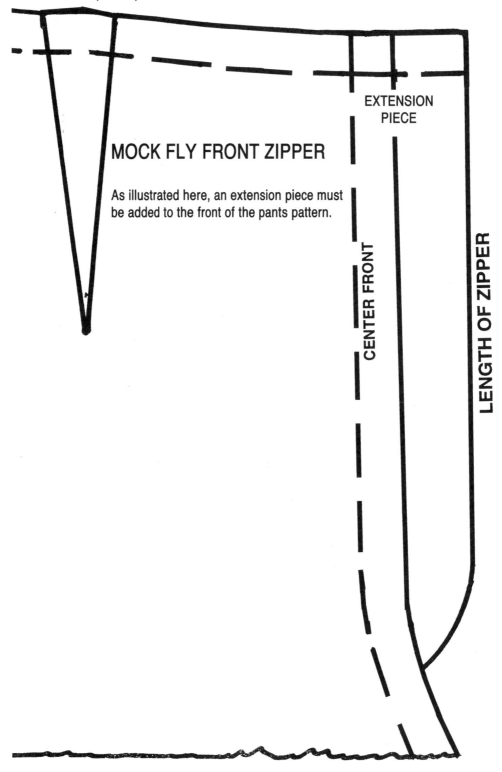

MOCK FLY FRONT ZIPPER

As illustrated here, an extension piece must be added to the front of the pants pattern.

EXTENSION PIECE

CENTER FRONT

LENGTH OF ZIPPER

SEWING INSTRUCTIONS FOR PANTS

Pants are always sewn with the same general sewing steps. The following method keeps the garment lying flat as long as possible. Illustrated are the step-by-step instructions for sewing any pant style. Follow the steps in a consecutive order - do not skip around. The sequence begins after the pattern has been laid out on the fashion fabric, cut properly, and all pattern markings have been transferred to the fabric.

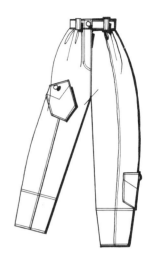

1   ATTACH ANY INTERFACINGS
(This would include all waistbands or facing areas that need to be reinforced.)

Two methods are used to attach interfacing:
A The machine-basting method in which a non-fusible interfacing is machine-stitched 1/8 inch from the seam's outer edge.

B The pressing method in which the glue-coated side of a fusible interfacing is placed to the wrong side of the garment and fused in place with a steam iron.

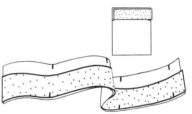

2   SEW ANY DARTS, GATHERS, TUCKS , OR PLEATS ON EACH SEPARATE PIECE
Check the pant pieces for any darts, gathers, tucks, or pleats. If there are no darts, gathers, tucks, or pleats, then skip this step.

DARTS:
A Fold the correct side of the fabric together, matching the dart legs (notches). If necessary, pin the dart line.

B Following the stitch line exactly, continue to stitch the dart from the wide end to the point. Backstitch both ends.

TUCKS:
A With the correct side of the fabric together, fold and match each leg (notches) of the tuck.

B Sew (and backstitch) from the top of the tuck to the bottom of the tuck. Stitch across the bottom to complete the tuck.

PLEATS:
A With the correct side of the fabric together, match the pleat notches to each other.

B Baste from the fold to the notches to hold the pleat in place until the waistband is attached.

SEW DARTS, TUCKS
OR PLEATS

3   SEW ALL STYLE LINES

Any vertical or horizontal seam line other than a waistline, inseam, or side seams is considered a style line. Most style lines usually run from the waistline to the hem or from side seam to side seam. Yoke seams are a very common styleline.

Match the notches and sew the style line seam.

GATHERING SEAMS FOR STYLELINE SEAMS:

Gathering is a method of pulling up basting stitches to make the fabric fit into a smaller space. An entire seam or a distance between two specific points may need to be gathered.

A Sew two rows of basting stitches at the area specified.

B Pull the bobbin threads until the garment piece is the needed length.

C Stitch the gathered section to the adjoining seam

4   STITCH FRONT AND BACK BACK CROTCH SEAMS.

A Matching correct side to correct side, stitch the center back crotch sections together.

B Stitch the front crotch sections together. Start stitching from the area where the zipper will be sewn and continue down to the inseam.

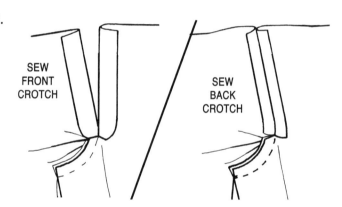

SEW FRONT CROTCH

SEW BACK CROTCH

IF A ZIPPER IS TO BE INSERTED:

Press the seam allowance for the zipper to the inside of the pants.

5   INSERT ZIPPERS AT CENTER FRONT OR CENTER BACK.

NOTE: If there is a side seam zipper, these same steps should be followed after the side seam area is sewn. To sew a side seam zipper, use 1 inch seam allowance and topstitch 1/2 inch from the folded seam edge.

A Place the pant correct side up. Working on the left seam allowance, slide out and pin this seam allowance 1/4" beyond the pressed seam line.

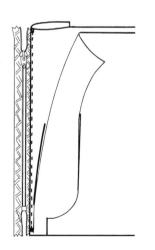

B Close and place the zipper correct side up. Position one edge of the zipper teeth next to the extended seam allowance of the pant. Pin in place.

C Using a zipper foot and starting from the bottom of the zipper, stitch close to the folded edge of the seam allowance the entire length of the zipper.

D With the correct side of the garment facing up, pin the other seam allowance over the closed zipper so that it conceals the zipper and the other top stitching.

E Turn the pant wrong side up. Stitch the zipper tape to the fly extension only.

F Machine stitch 3/4" parallel to the fly fold through all layers of the fabric, curving to meet the bottom of the zipper.

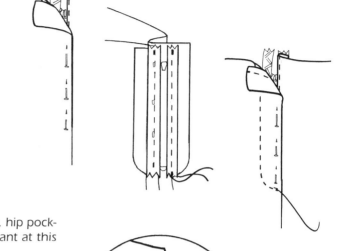

6 SEW THE POCKETS

While the garment is relatively flat, in-seam pockets, hip pockets, or any patch pocket should be sewn to the pant at this time.

IN-SEAM POCKETS:

Sew the pockets to the side seams.

A With the top of each pocket 1 inch below the waistline, pin one pocket section to the front at each side seam. Place correct sides together, matching side seam raw edges.

B Stitch the seam from the top of the pocket to the lower edge of the seam.

C Press the pocket seam allowances at the side seam toward the pocket.

PATCH POCKETS:

Mark the exact position of the pocket on the correct side of the garment before attaching the pockets.

A Edgestitch the top of the pocket.

B Turn and pin the facing area of the pocket along the facing foldline, correct side to correct side.

C Stitch the pocket facing area along the seam line on the pocket edge. Trim the facing corners.

D Turn and press the facing and the seam allowance to the inside, folding the seam allowance along the stitchline.

E Pin the pocket onto the pants at the marked pocket location, matching wrong side of the pocket to the correct side of the pants. Topstitch the pocket to the pants, using the edge of the presser foot as a seam guide.

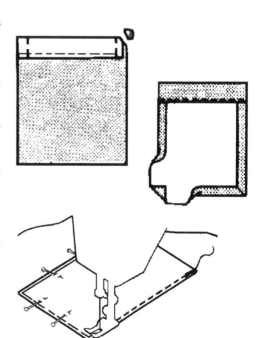

HIP POCKETS:

A Pin and stitch the top pocket to the pant section, matching correct side to correct side. Trim the pocket seam, leaving 3/8" seam allowance.

B Understitch the seam allowance to the pocket facing by extending the pocket section out. Position all the seam allowances toward the pocket. On the correct side of the pocket, machine stitch close to the seam line. While stitching, gently pull the fabric on both sides of the stitchline so the fabric lies flat.

C Turn the pocket to the inside and press.

D Pin the under pocket to the top facing along the pocket curved edges, matching correct sides.

E Flip curved edge of pocket away from the pants. Stitch the top pocket and the under pocket around the curved edges.

F Pin the pocket in place, matching the waistline and the side seam.

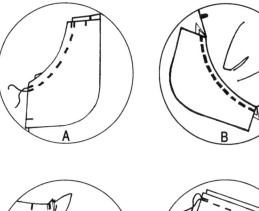

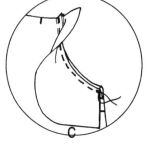

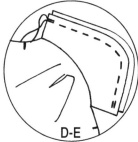

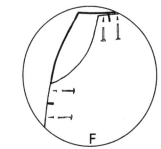

7   SEW THE SIDE SEAMS.

Place the front and back pant sections to each other, matching the seams accurately, correct side to correct side. Stitch from the top of the seam down to the hem edge.

If the pant has side seam pockets, stitch from the top of the seam down to the bottom of the seam, following around the shape of the pocket. Clip the side seam allowance above and below the pocket.

8   SEW THE IN-SEAMS.

Place the front and back inseams to each other, correct sides together. Stitch from the crotch seam down on both pant legs.

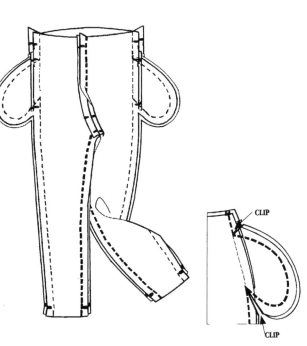

9 ATTACH WAISTBANDS or WAIST FACINGS

WAISTBANDS:

A Fold the waistband in half lengthwise, matching correct sides.

B Stitch one end closed with the correct seam allowance. Stitch the extension end closed with the correct seam allowance. Trim the corners.

C Turn the waistband correct side out.

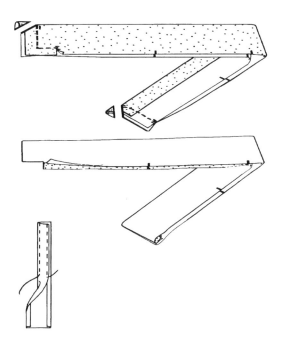

OPTIONAL BELT CARRIERS

1 Press under 3/8" on long edge of belt carriers. Fold carrier in half lengthwise, with WRONG sides together. Stitch close to both long edges as shown. Cut the strip into four equal lengths.

2 With CORRECT sides together, pin carriers to upper edge of the pant, placing them centrally over the front and back darts. Baste in place.

D With the garment side facing up, pin the correct side of the waistband (one layer only) to the wrong side of the garment. Match the following positions:
- Center back of the waistband to the center back of the garment.
- Side seams of the waistband to the side seams of the garment.
- Center front of the waistband to center front of the garment.

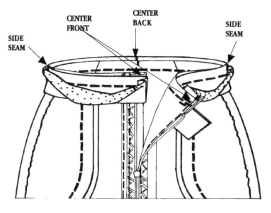

CENTER FRONT   CENTER BACK   SIDE SEAM   SIDE SEAM

E With the correct side of the garment facing up, machine-stitch the pinned garment to the waistband.

F Turn the waistband to the correct side of the garment. Pin the interfaced side of the waistband (with the folded-under seam allowance) over the stitchline.

G From the outside of the garment, edgestitch the waistband along the folded-under seam allowance. Stitch through all thicknesses the entire length of the waistband.

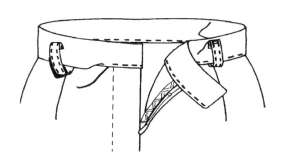

FINISH BELT CARRIERS (OPTIONAL) Press belt carriers upward onto the waistband, turning under 3/8" on raw edges. (Allow a bit of ease from the top to the bottom of the belt carrier.) Topstitch belt carrier securely.

SEW A WAIST FACING:
A facing may be used to clean finish a waist area instead of a separate waistband or a waist casing.
NOTE: Interfacing for the waist facing area should already have been applied in STEP 1.

A   Edgestitch or overlock the lower edge of the facing.

B   Sew the facing front side seams to the facing back side seams.

C   Pin the correct side of the facing to the correct side of the pant, matching the waist seam cut edges. Match:
- Center back of the facing to the center back of the pant.
- Side seams of the facing to the side seams of the pant.
- Center front of the facing to the center front of the pant.

D   With the correct side of the garment facing up, machine-stitch the pinned facing to the pant, using the required seam allowance.

E   Press the entire seam allowance toward the facing. Understitch the waist seam to keep the facing seam from rolling out. This is achieved by extending the facing out flat and folding all seam allowances to the facing side. From the correct side of the facing, stitch through the facing and seam allowance 1/8" from the seam line.

F   Turn the facing to the wrong side of the pant and press. Hand stitch the facing to the side seam and the center opening seam. At the top of the facing where the garment opening is located, hand stitch a hook and eye to help secure the waistline.

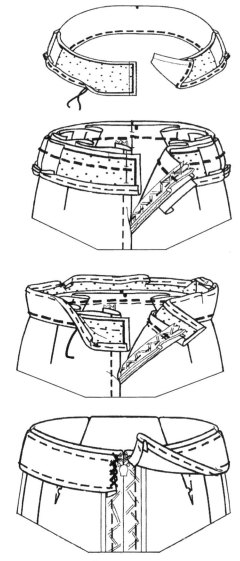

10 FINISH ALL HEMS.
Press up hem allowances. Baste to hold in place. Slip-stitch or catch stitch hem in place.

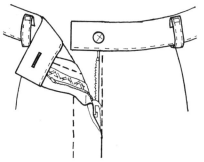

11 CHOOSE A CLOSURE FOR THE GARMENT.
Make the buttonhole on the correct section of the waistband. (Right side for women's, Left side for Men's) Lap ends and sew button under the buttonhole.

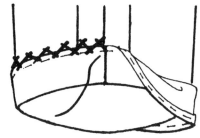